Fight Naked

Fight Naked

More True Stories
to Make You Laugh

Kathy Thorson Gruhn

For information about other books or performances,
go to: kathythorsongruhn.com
or
mybabycompass.com

Layout and editing by Maureen Ryan Griffin
Cover Photo by Stephen Reisch

Manufactured in the United States
MBC Publishing
289 Green Fields Lane
Columbus, NC 29722

ISBN 978-0-9844085-6-6
ISBN 0-9844085-6-8 (eBook)

for my grandchildren –
Miles, Eden, and Waylon

Table of Contents

Introduction

If you read my first book, *Drug Tested for Being Happy*, you know that I love to see people laugh. In fact, when Jack Canfield, creator of the *Chicken Soup for the Soul* series, heard me tell a few of my funny stories at a conference, he insisted that I put them in a book and perform them. There wasn't enough clean humor in the world, he said, and my stories were some of the funniest he'd ever heard.

I had such a great time writing the first book, and so many people asked for more stories, that I wrote a second one, in the same format. Some of these stories are about my husband, Bill. I wrote them to help me get through the sadness I felt as my husband was dying. These stories made me laugh and remember the crazy times we had together. I have changed some names and places to protect the not so innocent.

When Bill was in the hospital and then in hospice care, he looked forward to hearing whatever funny story I'd written each week. Laughing eased the pain of his inevitable death. Sometimes a nurse would overhear my storytelling and join us. When the laughter subsided, the next thing I would hear was, "Is that true?" Bill and I would look at each other, nod our heads, and begin to laugh all over again.

I call the stories in *Fight Naked*, like the ones in *Drug Tested for Being Happy*, true stories, because I have to convince people that they really happened even though they sound improbable or ridiculous. I don't know how I get myself into so many predicaments, but fortunately, I have great angels, with a good sense of humor, who have helped me survive them!

Not only did I listen to Jack Canfield and put my stories in a book, but I'm also performing them on stage. I play my Dobro while my brother, Ty, plays the guitar. People call our shows "Piedmont Home Companion" because of the blend of music and stories, my Minnesota heritage, and the "Ole and Lena" jokes I tell. All of this is a far cry from my previous career as a speech pathologist, but I enjoy it just the same.

One of the best things about this new career of mine is getting so many emails, phone calls, and comments by people who read *Drug Tested for Being Happy*. They tell me that they laughed out loud and had fun sharing the stories with family and friends. I hope *Fight Naked* brings more laughter to the world. Researchers say that children laugh approximately 154 times a day, while adults only laugh 14 times a day. What happened? Why the shortage of laughter in adults? Are we too busy? Too uptight? Do our funny cells die out?

Scientists have discovered that laughter not only lifts our spirits, but also boosts our immune system. Obviously, we all need more laughter—I'm working on that. Enjoy!

Fight Naked

On a beautiful April day in North Carolina, with the azaleas and dogwood trees in full bloom, my friend, Christi, and I walked around a horse show at Lata Park Plantation near Charlotte, North Carolina. We placed our chairs next to the ring under the shade of a live oak tree to watch the children's division. We enjoyed the view as young riders trotted their ponies over cross rails in the warm-up arena. When the medium pony division started, the first pony into the ring caught my eye, and Christi's, too.

"Look at that pony. Oh, it's so cute. Pretty mover. I wonder if it's a good jumper," she said.

"I was thinking the same thing. What a good-looking gray. Those dapples are precious."

The pony, Rosie, won her under saddle class. When she entered the ring for the jumping class, her ears were perked and her rhythm was steady. She cantered around the course of eight jumps, easily executing a flying lead change. She won the medium pony division and was awarded a blue ribbon along with a grand champion ribbon.

"Did you see how tight her knees were when she went over that fence? Not only is she a good mover, but a great jumper," Christi said.

"I couldn't agree more," I said.

"Your daughter needs a pony like that."

"Ya, sure, in your wild dreams. Jennifer has Toby."

"A five-hundred-dollar, stubborn appaloosa. What's she going to learn on him? How to be frustrated?" Christi said.

"He is a challenge."

"Challenge? He does trail rides, but he doesn't do ring work. At the last pony club schooling, the poor girl had to have someone grab the reins and drag him away from the gate. She couldn't get him to enter the riding ring."

"Ya, I know. Maybe he'll come around."

"In your dreams," Christi said.

"Let's look at Dover's tack trailer. I need some tack cleaning supplies," I said, changing the subject.

As we were heading for the trailer, we saw the gray pony, Rosie. Christi walked over to the lady who was leading her.

"What a cute pony. How old is she?" Christi asked.

"She's eight. Are you interested in buying her? She's for sale."

Christi looked at me. I looked right back. Then I walked over to the pony.

"She sure is a good jumper. How much are you asking for her?"

"She's a Welch Hills pony and I have a trainer, Jack Towel, coming to look at her. She's nine thousand dollars."

I almost choked and started laughing. "I've never spent more than a thousand dollars for a horse in my life. I'm sure Jack will love her."

Giving Christi a ride home from the horse show, she started in as soon as we got in the car.

"You should get that pony," she said. "Let Jennifer ride her for a few years and you'll be able to get your money back out of her because she's young. I think you'll regret it if you don't buy her."

"And where will I get nine thousand dollars? Really? You know we live paycheck to paycheck."

"I work for a bank. You can get a loan."

"Don't tempt me."

"You're working and you would qualify," she said.

"Bill would kill me. That's more than we paid for both our cars put together."

"How would your hubby know? He doesn't have to sign the loan. It can be in your name. Use your car as collateral," Christi said.

"Really? You think so?"

"I know so."

The next day I called the woman and told her I wanted to buy Rosie. I went to the bank, took out a loan, and bought her. Christi and I laughed all the way to my barn as we towed Rosie in my horse trailer to her new home.

I pulled it off. I told Bill the pony belonged to someone else and he believed me.

I was feeling pretty good until a few days later, when I came home and saw Bill on the phone.

He hung up and turned around to face me. "Is there anything you want to tell me?"

"No," I said, as innocently as possible. "Why?"

"I just got off the phone with the bank. It seems your loan papers are ready."

I froze. Busted! I didn't know what to say.

"I think you have some explaining to do." Bill's eyes were turning into small slits and his lips were getting tighter.

"I bought the gray pony. But don't worry, we'll get our money back out of her in a few years. She's young and very talented," I pleaded. "And Jennifer needs her."

"You took out a loan without talking to me. I can't believe you lied to me."

Bill's face was beet red. I had no excuse. There was no way I could reason with him. He was right. I had lied, and he was spitting mad. I didn't know what to do.

Then I remembered our huntsman, Mr. Russel, saying that a man can only think of one thing at a time. I started dancing around singing the melody of a strip tease song as I took my clothes off. Bill kept yelling at me, but I kept right on singing and dancing until I was down to my bra and underwear.

"Put your clothes back on. Your little trick isn't going to work with me," he said.

I stopped, gave him a dirty look as I felt the tears building, and blurted out, "No problem. I will! I told you I was sorry. I told you I would pay for everything until I sold her. I'm working fulltime. This isn't for me. It's for our daughter." I wiped away the tears, put on my clothes, and headed for the door.

"Where're you going?" he asked.

"What do you care? I'm out of here." I grabbed my purse, slammed the door, and headed for the car.

I went to Christi's house, told her what happened, and cried.

"Let's go for lunch," she said.

I told her that I was in really hot water and I felt so guilty. She apologized for encouraging me to buy the pony, but insisted that I wouldn't regret it.

After lunch, I reluctantly headed home, dreading the fact that I would have to face Bill. He came to the door as I walked into the house.

"I'm so sorry I yelled at you. Can you forgive me? You're right. You can pay for the pony and then sell her to get your money back. You have that right. You're working and you should be able to make decisions independently, but don't ever lie to me again. Okay?" he said, as he hugged and kissed me.

"Are you being nice to me because you were thinking about what you were missing?" I asked, looking him straight in the eye.

"A little. Well . . . a lot," he said. "Why don't we start where you left off before you went out the door, okay?"

Bless Mr. Russel for reminding me a man has a one-track mind.

A few weeks later, Bill and I attended a wedding. When the ceremony was over, the wedding planner shoved the microphone in my face and asked, "What advice do you have for the newly wedded bride?"

"Fight naked," I said in all seriousness. "You see, a man can only think of one thing at a time. If you're having an argument, start disrobing and see what happens. If he can't stop fighting, go have lunch with your girlfriend and let him think about what he's missing. I'm not sure how many times it'll work. I only tried it once."

Years later, this is still my best advice when it comes to marriage. No quick-fix program, self-help book, or even magic wand will solve the age-old problem of 'two points of reality.' And, sometimes, a compromise just can't be found.

In or out of marriage, humor can solve many small and some large problems. Being able to laugh at yourself and laugh at the circumstances can really help when times are tough. There is nothing to lose and much to gain from taking ourselves a little less seriously, having more fun, and laughing as often as possible.

I hope these silly but true stories will place a smile on your face, provide you with some fodder to share with others, and encourage you to think of your own foibles and follies as opportunities for laughter.

Have a great day and, the next time you're in a pinch with your romantic partner, remember my advice, *FIGHT NAKED.*

Growing Up in
Blooming Prairie

Is It Genetic?

Sometimes I wonder if there's a humor gene. Do some families laugh more than others? I believe I inherited my penchant for mishaps, and for laughter, from my father's side of the family. Everyone told funny stories at family gatherings. These were usually about a relative, but many times, they were at the expense of the person telling the story. Let me give you a few examples of what I'm talking about.

My Dad, Glenn Thorson

Although my father had a great sense of humor, that is not the first thing people thought about when they heard his name. He was a good lawyer, but he was also a strong believer in helping children and the disadvantaged. Community was an important concept and he gave fifty percent of his earnings back into developing a better living for everyone. He helped build a Boy Scout camp, a golf course, a swimming pool, a nursing home, and churches of all faiths, in addition to sending underprivileged students to college.

When the depression hit our small rural area, my father bought the land from local farmers for a dollar, helped pay the bills, and when they got back on their feet, he sold the farms back to their original owners for the same amount, one dollar. He had the opportunity to become very rich, but that wasn't his goal in life. His passion was helping others. My father never boasted about any of this, or even talked about it. I had to learn about his generosity from the people he helped.

And his humor? Well, it was often sarcastic, and, at times, he used it to make a point. A close friend of the family, Delph Marcott, reminded me of one such instance while Blooming Prairie was in the process of building a new elementary school. The story goes like this:

Our local parents who had children with special needs had to drive over ten miles to another school that could accommodate them. Traveling this distance wasn't an easy task in the winter in southern Minnesota. My father was on the school board and the planning committee. Delph, nick-named Babe, had a child that was mentally challenged. She approached my father to ask if an extra classroom could be built for these children.

At the school planning board meeting, my father said, "I believe we should add an extra classroom for students in our community who have mental and physical challenges. It's difficult for these parents to drive out of town in the winter and one extra classroom and teacher won't break the budget."

"That isn't necessary," the president of the local bank shot back. "The children are being taken care of. Anyway, they aren't going to be able to hold down jobs or be tax-paying citizens. Why do they need an education?"

"Oh, I disagree with you on that. It wouldn't be difficult to train them to become president of the local bank!" my father said with a bite in his voice.

That was the end of the bank president's objections. The classroom was built and the parents of the special needs children were happy.

He was named Mr. Blooming Prairie in 1967, and an honorary dinner was given at the First Lutheran Church. At the award's presentation, he listened to Mr. James Mork name all of his accomplishments. He was given the microphone to say a few words and this was his response: "You've heard my eulogy, now you can view the remains." Everyone had a good laugh.

My family was proud when my dad was selected as Outstanding Senior Citizen for the state of Minnesota in 1972 by the State Fair Board and supported by Governor Wendell Johnson. His picture is posted, along with other candidates, on a wall in a building at the fairgrounds in the Twin Cities.

My Aunt Ruby

My aunt Ruby, my dad's younger sister who lived in Wisconsin, was famous for her funny stories. We would see her once in a while, along with her family. She had dark brown eyes and dark brown hair. It seemed like everyone I knew in my small town had blue eyes and blonde hair, and so, whenever I saw Ruby, I would stare at her brown eyes. This would make her laugh.

My favorite of all her stories happened while she was on vacation in Connecticut. She was standing at the counter of an ice cream store when she heard the soft ring of a bell as someone entered the store. She turned around and there was Paul Newman, the famous actor—and her heart throb. She was, as Lena and Ole would say, as nervous as a long-tailed cat in a room full of rocking chairs as Mr. Newman stood in line right behind her.

Ruby didn't know if she should say hi to Mr. Newman, ask for his autograph, or give him privacy. She was conflicted. She really wanted to talk to him and tell everyone that she met and talked to Paul Newman, but she was too shy to say anything. "I'll have a chocolate ice cream cone," she said to the girl behind the counter.

"Here you go and here's your change," the girl said, handing the cone to Ruby.

When she got outside, she realized she didn't have her ice cream cone. Ruby went back into the store and again, she was conflicted. Should she interrupt Paul Newman while he was ordering? Would he think she was stalking him?

But she couldn't have her ice cream cone melt. So, she bravely went up to the counter, stood right next to him and said, "Excuse me. I left my ice cream cone here, and I came back to get it."

Paul Newman leaned into her. She froze, totally taken aback. Was he going to give her a kiss? Tell her a secret?

Then he whispered in her ear, "Your ice cream cone is in your purse."

My Aunt Elida

Dad's older sister, Elida, also lived in Wisconsin. She was tall and very Norwegian in her appearance and demeanor. When she was with my father, their presence dominated the room. On one of her visits, we were sitting around the dining room table after dinner laughing as Mom told stories about my brothers and Dad told tales about Mom's relatives. This was typical at our family gatherings. The boys didn't mind being the brunt of many of the funny stories and my mom, well, she would politely smile at my dad when he slipped in a story about her dad or one of her sisters. My dad helped her family financially and loved my mother very much. She knew he was a good man.

The story I remember from that evening was Elida's shoe shopping trip. She was with her sister, Viola. Elida was overweight and her legs and feet would swell. As the shoe salesman held out shoe after shoe for her, she strained to get her feet into them. All of a sudden, she passed gas—a loud fart!

"Excuse me, I'm really not interested in any shoes. I have to go," Elida said, completely embarrassed. Quickly putting her shoes on, she grabbed Viola, who I'm sure was giggling, and practically ran out of there with her sister in tow.

She soon realized she had left her purse at the shoe store. She had to get it and she was hoping she could go back in unnoticed. As she entered, she saw the same clerk who had waited on her. She figured he'd be the person who would have her purse. As hard as it was for her, she went up to him.

Elida was so nervous, and she said, "Excuse me. I left in such a hurry, that I forgot my fart."

"You mean your purse?" the salesman asked, smiling.

I'm sure Viola was in stitches the whole time the salesman was retrieving Elida's purse.

My Uncle Harvey and Aunt Kack

My aunt Kack was married to my dad's brother Harvey. She was a spunky lady and lived until age 96. However, Harvey lived even longer, until he was 104 years old. I asked him how it was to be so old, yet still so agile and mentally with it.

"Oh, it's a little rough. I had to give up golf, because those eighty-year-old whippersnappers couldn't keep up with me walking the course and I don't like using golf carts. I also had to give up my driver's license, because if there was an accident, I'd be blamed because of my age, not my driving ability," he said.

I never saw Harvey without Kack. They were a cute pair. Kack had a quick wit and she was so proper. They lived in Washington, D.C., and they bailed me out a couple of times. One of those was when my friend Denise and I had taken a bus from Mankato University to the United States capital to talk to Walter Mondale, our Minnesota senator, about the Vietnam War. Knowing that students didn't have much money, the organization sponsoring the event found a church that would house three busloads of students. Denise and I had our sleeping bags, but we didn't know we were supposed to bring our own food. We talked to Senator Mondale and went back to the church. Denise and I were hungry and decided to try to find a restaurant. We had only a couple of dollars between us. As we left the church, we found out quickly we were in a dicey part of town as we saw homeless people peeing on the church walls and drug addicts shooting drugs.

I called my Uncle Harvey for help and food. He parked blocks away for fear the car would be hijacked and he walked to the church. He picked us up and we stayed with them. He dropped us back off when the buses had to return to Minnesota. We slept in safety and comfort that night.

The other time Harvey and Kack bailed me out was many years later, when I was married to Bill, a physician, and we attended a rheumatology convention in Washington, D.C. We were visiting to introduce them to our two-year-old daughter, Alice, and to catch up on old times. I also wanted Bill to meet Harvey because he reminded me of my father, whom Bill had never met. Bill adored Harvey immediately. They talked about the war, politics, and Harvey's job at the Securities and Exchange Commission. They acted as if they'd known each other forever.

When Kack asked about the rheumatology convention, we mentioned that we were expected to go to a dinner and dance with the other physicians, but that we would miss the fun because we didn't have a babysitter for Alice.

"I'll take care of her," Kack said. I was surprised because Kack and Harvey didn't have any children of their own.

"Are you sure? She's a two-year-old," I said.

"No problem. She can spend the night. You two have fun and we'll see you tomorrow."

I couldn't believe it. It was the first night for me to be away from my toddler and I trusted Harvey and Kack completely. On our drive back to the hotel, Bill said, "That's so nice of your aunt and uncle to take care of Alice. How old are they anyway?"

"Let's see. Harvey maybe is 65...no...70. No...let's see. My dad was born in 1892 and Harvey I think was born in 1896...or maybe 97."

"It's 1982! You mean we have left our two-year old with two people who are almost 90 years old?" Bill asked, slamming on the brakes of the car. "Are you crazy? I know they don't look their age, but we should be looking after them!"

"Wait. I'm not going to go back there and tell them they can't take care of Alice because they're too old. How embarrassing. They offered to take care of her. They wouldn't suggest it if they didn't think they were capable."

"Okay, but we're going back first thing in the morning to make sure everything is okay."

The next morning, Bill couldn't get out of the hotel fast enough. I don't know if he thought Harvey and Kack would both be dead or what. I didn't say a word as I threw on my clothes.

It took a while for Harvey to answer the door. "You are early birds," he said. "It's only seven o'clock. Alice is still asleep in the bed with Kack."

I ran up the stairs and there was Alice, thumb in her mouth, rubbing the silky part of her blanket, cuddled up next to Kack.

"All is well," I said as I returned to a hot cup of coffee.

Kack came down the stairs a little later holding Alice's hand. "We had a great night and read ten of her books before bed. I repeated nursery rhymes and songs I remembered from my own childhood and that was a long time ago."

"Yes, a long time ago," Bill said as he gave me the 'look'.

"Do you have any stories?" I asked, quickly switching the subject as I packed Alice's things. I felt we had already taken advantage of their generosity.

"Oh, maybe a golf story," Kack said.

"Which one?" Harvey asked.

"The one when we went golfing with the prominent generals the other day," Kack said with a twinkle in her eye.

"I don't think it's appropriate for Dr. Bill Gruhn," Harvey said.

"Oh, he's heard worse from me, I'm sure. Tell it," I said, not looking at Bill.

"Well, we were out at the country club and we had two top generals with us," Kack began. "I won't tell you their names to spare them any embarrassment. We were on the seventh hole and we were about to get back in the golf cart when I noticed that the general hadn't zipped up his golf bag and he was about to lose things out of it. So, I said, 'You better zip up or you're about to lose your balls.' The general looked down and his pants were unzipped. 'Oh thanks,' he said as he zipped up his pants. I gave him a look and said, 'I didn't mean your pants. I was talking about your golf bag.'"

"Oh my," I said, laughing partly at the story and partly at the sound of Kack cackling away with a voice that had weakened with age. Bill and Harvey couldn't help themselves as they joined in.

I was still laughing as I thanked them for taking care of Alice and we headed out the door on our way back to the hotel.

Yes, I'm waiting for researchers to discover the humor gene. Until then, I'll just assume it's half nature and half nurture.

Mom, the Seamstress

The antique Singer sewing machine that my mom used is now in my daughter's Airbnb in Asheville, North Carolina, serving as a makeup table. Who knows how long it's been since anyone lifted up the tabletop, flipped the machine until it was locked in an upright position, and threaded the machine's needle to sew something? The pedal that ran the motor and controlled the speed was attached under the table, requiring the use of your knee. It worked fabulously.

When I was growing up, it was a treat to go to the dime-store and find a new Simplicity pattern for my next outfit. I could pick out my own material and have an original dress, blazer or skirt. Going clothes shopping at a department store was a rare occurrence. We had to drive to another town. The only other store in Blooming Prairie besides Woolworths was Harriet's Dresswell Shop, and their merchandise appealed to my mom's generation.

I can remember Mom—Isabelle, also known as Izzy—sitting at the sewing machine with her glasses on, an intense look on her face. She would hit the pedal and run that machine at full speed. Exactly the same way she typed. Full speed. She'd tell me, "I get a lot done. I'm fast and 95%

correct, which is still an A." Then, there was me. In the beginning, I was slow and a perfectionist, with 100% accuracy. But I didn't get nearly as much done. Now, I have my mom's philosophy: full speed ahead.

My mom experienced the Depression, which had a lasting effect on her. I have a picture of her wearing a dress her mother sewed for her when she was eight years old. It looked as if it were made from feed sacks. My mom owned one pair of shoes, and she lived in a two-room cabin in northeastern Montana, along with her father and three siblings. Her mother died of pneumonia a few years after that picture was taken. My eleven-year-old mother was sent to Blooming Prairie, Minnesota, to live with relatives along with her older sister, Viola. Her oldest brother and sister, Ronny and Evie, stayed back to help with the farm work.

Izzy was ahead of her time and became a fashion-conscious lady later in life. She was the first one in Blooming Prairie to wear shorts. She made the pattern herself. They were mid-thigh in length, baggy, and would probably be classified as culottes rather than shorts these days. When she walked down the street with her beautiful legs in full view, the men slowed down their cars and trucks (not whistling because that would've been rude). This is not why my mom wore the shorts . . . it was for comfort's sake. She was too shy, pious and pure in thought to attempt to gain attention. She didn't have a vain bone in her body.

My mom was a good seamstress, but some of her sewing ideas presented a problem for me. I believe her Depression experience had an influence. Like when I outgrew my one-piece swimsuit, and she decided to make it into a two-piece. I was twelve at the time and just starting to notice how cute the neighbor boys were getting. My dad, who built and ran the community pool, opened it up early that year because we had a hot spell. I rushed home from school the first day to change into my swimsuit, and discovered it had been cut into two pieces. I put it on anyway and ran to the pool.

When I got there, I noticed Greg Hanson was standing in the water getting ready to swim to the deep part. I threw off my towel and stuck my foot in the water, pretending it was so cold that I wasn't sure I wanted to go in. This was my way of flirting with Greg, who was three years older than I was. I actually wanted him to pick me up and throw me in (a twelve-year-old's concept of a relationship). It was fun.

He kept looking at me and snickering as I swished my toe and smiled back. Then I noticed that he was staring at my chest. When I looked down at my suit, I saw two, little brown spots showing just above my swimsuit. The top of my two-piece was on backwards and wasn't covering what should have been covered. I was devastated.

I grabbed my towel and ran back to the house. I blamed the whole problem on my mom, because there wasn't a tag in the back of the top so I would know which side was which. She offered to sew in a tag, but I begged until she bought me a new suit. I couldn't look at the old suit without remembering that horrible incident. I was completely flat and still wearing undershirts, but the thought of Greg seeing my brown spots was too much for me to handle.

That was bad enough. My mother's cost-cutting, seamstress ways really caused problems when she decided to save money on my pantyhose. I was a tomboy and I snagged my nylons on a regular basis. Pantyhose, the new rage, were expensive compared to the individual nylons that you wore with a garter belt. I didn't like the buttons on the garter belt showing through my tight bell bottom pants, like the ones Cher wore. My mom reluctantly paid the $1.69 in the 1960s for pantyhose. I was her only daughter, after all.

As usual, I woke up at eight in the morning for school and went to my underwear drawer, only to find that my mom had sewn regular nylons to every pair of underwear I owned.

"Mom! What the. . ." I screamed. I was a teenager with a mouth by this time. Fifteen years old to be exact. She came running to my room expecting death.

"What is with my underwear?" I asked.

"It'll save us money. Every time you snag a nylon, we'll just cut it off and resew a new one onto your panties. I figure we'll save a dollar for each snagged leg."

"I'm not wearing this on gym day, so you're going to have to take off some of these nylons."

"No problem. They're attached with a simple slip stich and I can remove them with a snip. Pull the thread and voilà. It's gone!" Her smile indicated she was very proud of herself.

"I just don't know about this. Are you sure it'll work?"

"Yes, totally. Be brave and try it. You may start a craze," she said.

I put on her underwear/pantyhose creation and was out the door with just enough time to make it to my first class.

As I ran down the sidewalk in front of the school, the nylons started to tug on my underwear. This was the day of miniskirts and the hem on my dress was even with the bottom of my thumbs when my arms were stretched alongside my thighs. It was short, to say the least. I could feel my underwear sliding down my legs.

I slowed to a walk, trying to hold my underpants up by squishing my thighs tightly together. Half the high school could see me out the classroom windows, walking up to the side door of the school like a waddling duck. I was humiliated. My nylons were bagging around my ankles, and I knew my underwear was showing below my skirt. I managed to get to the door and quickly lifted up my skirt to hike up my underwear before entering the school. I knew I couldn't make it through the day, so I went straight to the office.

"You're late, Kathy," Mr. Nelson, the principal, said. He was tall, with a blondish, gray crew-cut and a bulging tummy. There was usually a grin on his face that made you smile back. But not today.

"I know, but it isn't my fault. My mom sewed nylons to all of my underwear and it isn't working. She has this idea that the Depression is going to hit again any day and she's trying to save money."

"Your mother is a paralegal and your father is a lawyer. I have a problem believing that. I'm calling your mom," he said.

"Good idea. Tell her to bring a different pair of underwear and to buy some pantyhose."

Mr. Nelson walked over to the phone and paused as if he was making an idle threat.

"Call her. Please," I begged.

"Hello, Mrs. Thorson. Your daughter is in my office, late for class, because she said her nylons are pulling down her underwear. I would like to hear your side of the story."

When he hung up the phone, I asked what my mom had said.

"She's on her way with the underwear and pantyhose. She also said that next time she'll buy queen-sized nylons because she forgot to allow for the distance from the bottom of the garter belt to the top of the leg," Mr. Nelson said, looking downward, as if he were reading a budget report. "I'll write you out a pass, but next time, it's detention."

"Don't worry. I'll be on time if I can keep my mom away from my panties and nylons."

I thought this was the end of Mom's nylon creations but I found out the hard way that she decided to sew up the runs in my pantyhose. Because the stiches were on the back of my leg, where I couldn't see them, I didn't realize this while I was putting my nylons on.

I found out when a student stopped me in the hall and asked me if I had had an operation. When I checked out the back of my left leg, I saw an eight-inch-long brown stripe in my nylons that looked just like sutures.

I went to the office, again. Very upset.

"Mr. Nelson, you need to call my mother. She messed with my nylons again."

"You're late for class and you expect me to believe another nylon story?"

"Look!" was all I needed to say as I turned around and showed him the 'sutures' on my leg.

"I don't believe this. Okay. Here's your pass," he said, working hard to keep a straight face.

There never was another nylon story, but . . . I was late for class a few more times with excuses just as crazy as these.

Over the Shoulder Boulder Holder

It was a spring morning during my eighth-grade year, and I woke up at my usual time, 8:10 a.m., to get to school by 8:30 a.m. (The school was about a half mile walk.) I slept as late as I could because I needed my beauty sleep, but I didn't care if my hair was combed or my clothes matched. With my usual haste, I flung open my dresser drawer, only to learn this wasn't a usual morning. There in its shiny, pink box was a brand-new, Maidenform Playtex brassiere. I had been begging for one for months, even though my chest looked like two raisins on a bread board. I wanted a bra like the other girls in my class. I took it out of the box and looked for the directions. There weren't any, and I had no idea how to put it on. I had four brothers and no sisters and Mom had already left for work and couldn't show me.

Clearly, I needed to take the bra apart. Bras in those days didn't have the convenient strap adjustment rings and sliders they have now. I carefully pushed the thin, cotton straps out of the plastic adjustment sliders that connected the straps to the front of the bra. The straps looked like the connectors on the straps of a backpack, except smaller and white. I wasn't sure how to thread the straps back through the bra's sliders when the time came, but I figured it couldn't be that hard.

I placed the cups in front of my chest and held them in place with my chin. With great difficulty, I reached around to my back and tried to get the two hooks into the two eyes, so the bra would stay on. The bra kept slipping and falling.

I pressed my chest against the wall to hold the bra in place and, with two hands, tried again to get the hooks into the eyes. No luck.

I went into the bathroom and looked in the mirror to try to line up the hooks and eyes, but I couldn't see them. Finally, I was able to catch one hook. That seemed to be enough to hold the bra together around my torso.

After much effort, I gave up trying to thread the straps back through the sliders. So, instead, I made a loop in the end of each strap and tied them to the plastic slider pieces on the front of the bra. I chose a sheer, white blouse to wear so every boy in the school would know I'd made the passage. I was wearing a bra!

Off I went to school feeling many years older and wiser.

"You're late!" my first-class teacher, Mr. Tashima, scolded me, pointing. "To the principal."

I walked into Mr. Nelson's office. "Sorry I'm late. I didn't know how to put on a bra. No one was there to show me," I said matter-of-factly. I had figured out that bringing up female matters solves any problem quickly, and usually with little drama.

"Are you telling the truth?" he asked. "I'm going to call your mom."

How many times did we have to go through this? "Call her. No problem," I said as I peered in the nurse's station to see who was faking an illness.

He must have been tired of calling my mother with undergarment-related questions. "Okay, this time I'll write you a pass, but next time it's detention," Mr. Nelson said. I had heard that before!

I walked back to class with a quick step, my head held high. I was glad to finally be a grown up so I didn't have to hear my girlfriends sing "You'll Be a Woman Soon" every time we had gym class. Today was going to be different.

Gym time arrived and we had to change into our gym clothes.

"I see you're wearing a bra."

One of my girlfriends had noticed! "Yah," I said, sucking in my stomach and sticking my chest out a little farther.

"You're starting out with the real thing. No training bra?"

"Nah. My girls don't need training. They're under control," I said not knowing what a training brassiere was, or understanding why my friends referred to their chest as 'girls'. I guess it was more eloquent than boobs.

When we started playing dodge ball, the bra was bugging me like crazy. It was tight and scratchy. I kept pulling at it while I was playing, and then I started rubbing up against the wall or rubbing my arms along my sides, so it didn't look so obvious. I was getting worried. How was I going to stand it? I still had half the school day to get through.

After class, we had to take our gym clothes off and shower. My girlfriends showered, dressed and were out the door in minutes. *How did they do that so fast?* I watched them hook their bras in the front and turn them around, but I didn't fully understand. How did they get their straps over their arms with the bra turned around? I didn't realize you could stick your arms through the straps, because I was still thinking you had to take the bra apart to get it on.

After my friends left, I struggled again with those straps, trying to weave them through those small, plastic sliders. I quickly gave up because I couldn't be late for class twice in one day. Looping the ends, I was able to tie the two straps to the plastic rings on the front of the bra. I had no idea that in my mad run to my next class, the straps came untied and fell over my shoulders and down the back of my blouse. Because I had nothing on my chest that needed to be held in place, I didn't feel anything different. There I was, galloping down the hall with bra straps flapping behind me like reins.

I made it just in time for Mr. Peterson's math class. I loved this class because, Greg, a boy I had a huge crush on, sat in the seat behind me. I was hoping he would see my new bra under my white shirt.

He saw it all right. Unbeknownst to me, he took the straps that were hanging out of the back of my blouse and tied them to the sides of my chair. I didn't feel a thing.

"Who would like to work the next problem on the board?" Mr. Peterson asked.

I raised my hand like the goody-two-shoes I was. As he looked around the room, my hand was waving so hard that it caught his attention.

"Okay, Miss Thorson, you can go to the board and work on the next problem."

I went to stand up and was immediately snapped back into my chair. I wiggled and squirmed, but I wasn't able to get up.

"I'm stuck. My blouse must be caught on the back of my chair," I said to Mr. Peterson.

The students behind me were snickering as Mr. Peterson slowly walked over to my desk and peered behind me.

"Hmmm," he said, "I think we have a problem here. I need to have you stay after class. I'll write you a pass. Ann, I want you to stay with her." Ann started to giggle. "And Greg, I'll see you in my office after class." Mr. Peterson gave the snickering kids the evil eye and the room went quiet. He walked slowly back to the blackboard in front of the room.

I whispered to Greg, "Just get my blouse unhooked from this chair."

"It's not your blouse. You're tied in by your bra straps," he whispered back.

My eyes widened and I felt my face flush. Embarrassing thoughts were racing through my head. *I'll have to move away. I'll never be able to face these people again. How will I ever live through this!*

After class, Ann graciously untied me. She was laughing so loud that I had to join in. Later on, in my high school years, I ended up dating Greg. I never brought up the bra story. I'm sure he remembered it, but he never brought it up, either. *Why?* Because I learned to comb my hair and match my clothes. Oh, and my chest wasn't two raisins on a bread board anymore.

Homecoming Debacle

When I was a senior in high school, I was elected to the Homecoming Court, along with four other girls. This was a big honor for a teenage girl who wasn't into fashion, make-up, or a lot of hoopla. I was also in charge of the Homecoming festivities including hiring the band.

Our football team was tough, and I'm not so sure this wasn't because of the name of our team: The Blossoms. Signs at our rival high schools read "Wilt the Blossoms," while ours said, "Flower Power." It was also a little unusual for a B squad to be called, "The Buds," and a C squad, "The Seeds." Our band was the Petal Tones and, of course, in the sixties, we were all flower children. It was a good fit. I liked it. The Blooming Prairie Blossoms. It was the brunt of a lot of jokes on *Prairie Home Companion*, but we liked the attention, and it didn't taint our reputation one bit.

Unfortunately, we were losing some of our players before the Homecoming game. Why? Well, one of the problems of living in a small town as a teenager is finding entertainment. This means creating your own, which, for some, means not making good decisions. There was always a kid who could grow a full beard and pass for twenty-one—and was willing to go into the liquor store and buy booze. Yes, sometimes we were known as Boozing Prairie rather than Blooming Prairie.

The weekend before Homecoming, there was a big, and I mean a huge party at a farmhouse a few miles out of town. My girlfriend, Rita, had told a few people that her mother wasn't home. That's all it took for hundreds of kids, and nearly as many kegs of beer, to show up. I didn't drink beer, but I loved to flirt and talk with all the boys in the crowd. Sometimes I would talk a guy into buying some Boone's Farm wine. Because it was so sweet, I couldn't drink much of that either.

On the night of the party, when I was leaving the Tastee Freeze, the local hangout, I noticed Rita was talking to some friends in a car. "Rita, what are you doing here? Don't you want to be at your farm for the party?" I asked.

"What party? What are you talking about?"

"Uh oh. The word is out that your mom isn't home and everyone is headed for your farm. And I mean everyone. Kegs of beer and all."

I barely finished my sentence before Rita jumped into a car and headed for her farm. My boyfriend and I followed her. We arrived and I couldn't believe the cars and masses of people. It was the largest party I'd ever seen. Everyone was outside, drinking from kegs and milling around. I jumped out of the car and started talking to the guys passing out the beer. My boyfriend got mad and we got into a big fight. He told me he was leaving, because I was flirting with the other boys. He was right and I asked him to take me home. I decided I would drive myself back to the party with my own car.

I don't know all the specifics, but when I tried to come back to the party, I stopped suddenly. There were flashing red lights in all directions from police cars. The party had been raided. All of a sudden, two kids came flying out of the cornfield and jumped into my car.

"Get out of here. There are cops everywhere. They're from three different counties. Freeborn, Mower and Steel. They're picking up kids in the cornfields and along the road. And they rounded up about a hundred kids at the party," one of the boys said, huffing and puffing after having run nearly a mile through a corn field. Out of nowhere, a policeman pulled up next to me. He rolled down his window and told us to get out of there or we would be arrested for loitering. I couldn't put the car in gear fast enough.

The next Monday was a sad day at the school. The news was that the cops rounded up the kids, took their driver licenses and told them to get back in their cars. The police had the kids drive in a caravan to the station in Albert Lea, (yes, the very people that they accused of drinking were driving) where they would be booked for underage drinking. I later heard that the lead police car slammed on the brakes when he saw a kid come out of the cornfield. This caused a bumper-to-bumper collision for some of the vehicles in line. No one was hurt, but many parents were unhappy when they saw their car. One of the guys, Craig, was lucky in that his older brother showed up at the station. A policeman was glad to get rid of a couple of kids, so he let Craig go, in addition to his friend Dave, and they weren't charged. The boys had a good laugh before they left as they watched one of their classmates, Stanley, steal a few swigs of whiskey from an unclaimed bottle when the police weren't looking. I guess he thought the party wasn't over. Many members of the senior class were at the party and it was a memorable moment for most.

I'm sure you've figured out by now that a couple of football players were at the party and were suspended from the game. It turned out okay, because they had fun hunting and fishing rather than tearing up their knees in football. The Homecoming ceremony still took place and I was crowned as Queen. I was lucky that I had gone home when I did, because I would have been pulled from the homecoming court. My angels were working overtime, as usual.

The night of the football game, I performed my majorette routine at half-time with my fire batons. Then it was time to ride on the back of a convertible around the football field with my homecoming crown and cape. The principal, Mr. Nelson, came over to tell me that the band from Minneapolis that I'd hired hadn't arrived yet. I wasn't concerned, because they had an hour and half drive and I didn't expect them early.

After the ride on the convertible, I headed over to our high school gymnasium. As I helped with the final decorations, I got nervous as I realized that in less than an hour, people would be arriving and the band was nowhere to be found.

I had met this African-American band, who played regularly at Minneapolis's First Avenue Bar, through a friend of my brother's. The music would be new to my small, lily-white hometown. I was so excited because Blooming Prairie had never seen a band from a large city that played blues and rock and roll. These boys were talented.

We had planned for a large crowd and were counting on selling a thousand dollars' worth of tickets, which would give our senior class a chunk of change. I tried calling the band on their land line number (remember, no cell phones back then!), but no one answered the phone. Yes, they were young, but I'd believed them when they assured me that they would be there.

Unfortunately, the band never did show. When the concert was about to start, I arranged for a friend to get my stereo and to ask everyone in the crowd if they could go back home and get all their records.

I told everyone they could come in for free and have a good time. It was fun seeing all the girls with backed-combed hair piled high in curls, fancy heels, chiffon dresses, wearing corsages that matched the boutonnieres pinned on the lapel of their boyfriends' tuxedos.

The only problem was that the stereo hadn't arrived yet and the homecoming court had to enter the gymnasium first. Everyone was getting antsy for the Grand Marshall parade so the party could begin. The King and Queen needed to lead with the rest of the homecoming court following. Luckily, I had a transistor radio. So, I found the station playing the best song and we started our march. But before we all made it inside, a commercial for car tires came on—Goodyear to be exact. We laughed, and I thought it was fitting. It turned out to be a "good year" for me, also.

Whatever happened to the band? Turns out they had the opportunity to play back up for the musician known as Prince, in Minneapolis. The lead band member called the school phone number, but there was no one in the office to answer. Cell phones weren't available at the time. I guess for the band it was a no-brainer. It would advance their musical careers. And for me? A great story!

Attending College
in Mankato

Creative Cooking

My mother was such a wonderful cook that I didn't see the need to learn. However, there came a day when I left home for college and I left my chef behind. This was a challenge, not because I couldn't cook, but because I discovered pizza, submarine sandwiches, donuts, candy and Chef Boyardee spaghetti, in addition to twenty extra pounds.

The dorm food didn't help either. It looked different every day, but tasted just the same. After a year in the dorm, I went to live with eight of my girlfriends in a house. That made learning to cook a necessity, as we took turns with the household chores, including preparing dinner. I called and asked my mom for her favorite recipes, because soon it was going to be my turn to cook.

"I don't measure anything, but I can give you the ingredients," she said.

"Well, how do I know how much of the ingredients to use?"

"Just go by how it feels, looks, smells . . . you know."

"I only know what it looks like when it's done and ready to eat."

"I'll give you my old Betty Crocker cookbook. You'll be fine."

That was what my mom would always say: "You'll be fine." I was worried. I waited patiently for the weekend so I could go home and pick up Betty. The Betty Crocker cookbook, that is. I always wondered if Betty really existed. I wanted to be on a first name basis.

When Friday came, I drove the sixty miles home to see family and bring back Betty. Mom handed me my first cookbook, *Betty Crocker's Picture Cook Book*. One step above a primer reader—it couldn't get any better. Learning through pictures. I could do that.

I couldn't believe how yellowed the pages were. Some were stained or slightly torn. I could tell which recipes were used most by the specks of spattered food on the pages. "Do I have to read this whole thing?" I asked. "I'm swamped with schoolwork."

"I'll help you start," Mom said, with a smile.

"Let's begin with boiling water," I said, with a laugh. "We can skip the measuring part. Mrs. Frederickson taught us that in Home Economics to an extreme. I know how to take a knife and tap down the flour and shave off the top. Same with the measuring spoons. Turning on the oven, setting the temperature and the timer is a no brainer. Let's get to the meat of the stuff. Literally to the meat," I said.

We turned to the meat section and Mom opened the page to preparing poultry. The first picture showed a knife cutting the breastbone, lifting out the backbone, and breaking major joints. I stared at it in horror, my mother's directions just a faint noise in the background.

"I can't do that. It's gross. I'm not attacking a chicken with a knife and breaking its arms and legs. It looks great when it's done, but I'll puke before I get there. Let's go to the desserts. I'd feel better starting there."

"That's not healthy. You need protein."

"I can open a can of something and heat it on the stove. Desserts, please."

We started on page 69 with Quick Breads. I leafed ahead all the way to page 250. I liked this book. It covered quick breads, yeast breads, cakes, frostings, cookies, pies and other sweet concoctions, and ended with frozen desserts. Wow! The pictures made me drool.

"I don't think starting with desserts is the best choice."

"Listen, Mom, I want to like cooking. I'll be motivated by sugar and butter. Trust me."

Mom put bookmarks in the pages with the recipes that she thought would be the easiest and gave me a few of her own that were separated by categories in an old wooden box with the word *Recipes* on the front. I was prepared to get back on the road to Mankato State University. All I had to buy was a rolling pin and baking sheets. Mom had given me everything else, including an apron. With my old jeans and t-shirts, I wasn't so sure I needed the apron.

My first conquest was banana bread. Since it was under Quick Breads, I thought it would be quick. It wasn't. I had to get to class, so I left the not-so-quick breads in the oven to bake while I was gone. The recipe said to bake 50 to 60 minutes. Close enough. When I got back home, there was a smoky smell. I looked in the oven and the breads weren't burned. I was so excited, I wrapped up the warm bread to bring to my next class.

I handed the loaf to the teacher. He thought it would be a great idea to share it with the class. I was so proud of myself. He set it on the table and took out his jackknife. He tried to cut it, then stabbed the bread. He wasn't able to penetrate the loaf. He tried again and the bread flew through the air and landed on the floor with a bang. It was as hard as a brick. Inedible.

Embarrassed, I headed back to the drawing board. This problem wasn't going to get the best of me. When in doubt, call Mom.

"Mom, you wouldn't believe what happened to me during my first baking experience," I said.

"Come home this weekend and watch me cook Thanksgiving dinner. I think that will be the easiest way for you to learn."

I watched and took notes of everything she did. I helped wherever I could. She handed me the turkey to place in the roaster. I didn't like the feel of the raw bird's body, so I grabbed the wings and danced with it, singing "The Chicken Dance." Mom didn't appreciate my creativity, but I learned how to cook poultry without having to attack it and rip it apart. I let Mom twist its wings and place the turkey on its back. I hadn't reached that comfort zone. After the turkey was in the oven, we continued with sticky buns, mashed potatoes, peas, dressing, gravy, sweet potatoes and cranberry cake with butter sauce. I loved making all of these and was sure I was well-prepared to cook Thanksgiving dinner myself.

I went back to school feeling I had finished my internship in food preparation. I also had the leftovers from our Thanksgiving dinner. I called a friend to come and share my meal.

"I want to make this cranberry cake with butter sauce," she said.

"No problem. It's easy."

I wrote down the recipe that Mom had scribbled for me and gave it to my friend. A couple of weeks later, she approached me while I was sitting at the table in the Union building.

"Have you had a chance to make the cranberry cake and butter sauce?" I asked.

"Yes, but it didn't turn out like yours. I don't know what I did wrong. When I started cooking the butter sauce, the next thing I knew, it was boiling over and I filled five containers with a bubbling, buttery froth. It tasted okay, but it looked weird."

It took me awhile to figure out what had gone wrong with my butter sauce recipe. It wasn't until I gave the recipe to another friend that I realized I had mixed up the thickening agent. I had told her to add two tablespoons of baking powder rather than cornstarch.

Oops! I guess I was a little overconfident.

Dog Gone It

With my mother's guidance, I learned to cook so well that I decided to grow herbs. I filled flowerpots with rosemary, thyme, lavender, sweet lemongrass, and different types of parsley that I used in my recipes. I took classes at school and progressed from Midwestern meat and potatoes to Indian and Italian cuisine.

When I left Mankato State University for the summer break, I continued to perfect my skills. I signed up for a wild mushroom hunting experience that required me to go into the woods with a guide. There were eight excited beginners in the class.

The day finally arrived for my trek into the wild. As we followed the guide through the woods, the other participants became competitive. It was like watching a flock of birds go after a piece of bread. Someone would spot a mushroom and the whole group would run to check it out. Most of the time it turned out to be poisonous. That's when I questioned whether this was a good idea. You could die eating a wild mushroom? Really?

Following the guide, to whom I was stuck like glue, so I wouldn't get trampled or lost, I was able to identify different mushrooms. I took pictures and made notes about the terrain where the mushrooms were located. After hours of hunting, we found hen of the woods, chanterelles, and the most prized variety, morels. The morels, known for their rich flavor, had honeycomb caps that were round, oval, or conical in shape.

When our time out in the woods was over, the guide prepared the mushrooms over a campfire. The morels were quite tasty, but we only found enough to make a meal for one person, so we each had a tiny morsel to try. The other mushrooms tasted like soggy sponges. "You add spices and a sauce," I was told. I didn't quite get it. You can do the same thing with egg noodles and they're no trouble at all to find! Oh, well, I was here to learn.

While we were tasting a variety of wild mushrooms, our guide told us a story about one of his students. I've never forgotten it. With the crackling fire and everyone in a circle, I felt as if I was back in Girl Scouts listening to ghost stories. I still haven't recovered from hearing about the man with the hook for a hand that would kidnap you if you went parking with your boyfriend. Maybe that was a ploy by the Girl Scout leaders so we would behave. I'm still not sure.

The mushroom guide began his story. "An older woman, I think she was around sixty, decided to take my class. A wealthy and distinguished member of the community, she took pictures of the mushrooms, labeled them, noted the location and what time of year they were available. She took two more classes to make sure she was able to go out on her own to find wild morel mushrooms. She was confident she knew what she was doing."

I was getting the feeling that this story wasn't going to end happily. Maybe I was having a Girl Scout flashback. I told the person next to me that I was full and he could finish the rest of my mushrooms. He ate them happily as the guide went on with his story, not looking at any of us. He stared into the fire pit as if he were reliving the incident himself. I looked around and everyone was chowing down. Obviously, I was the only one who had any reservations.

"After she'd collected a variety of wild mushrooms, she invited her friends for a dinner at her house to impress them with her new hobby," the guide said. "I imagine the table was set with linens, silver, and place cards for each of her guests. After she cooked the wild mushrooms, to be on the safe side, she fed a little to her husband's dog. Then she gave specific instructions to her maid, who was assisting her in serving the dinner guests. 'If anything happens to the dog, I want you to interrupt the dinner and let me know immediately.' She didn't explain why or tell the maid that she fed the dog some of the mushrooms. The maid agreed to do as she was told.

"The invited guests were finishing up the second course when the maid brought out the wild mushroom pasta dish.

"'Oh, my, what's this?' one of the guests asked.

"'These are wild morel mushrooms,' the hostess said. 'Highly desirable and expensive. I've been taking mushroom hunting classes with a guide, and I know how to identify and where to find them.'

"She explained her technique, how long she had been hunting mushrooms, and the fact that some types of mushrooms were poisonous. She assured them that these mushrooms were fine. Everyone cleaned their plate and a few of the guests had more than one helping. As they were waiting for dessert, the maid came in, leaned over the hostess and cupped her hand to the woman's ear.

"'The dog is dead,' she whispered."

My group of mushroom hunters looked up from their plates. All you could hear were the sounds of the forest. All eating and whispering had stopped. Now I felt we were on the same page. *Where was this story going? Did he not realize we were eating these very mushrooms?* I was beginning to feel queasy.

The guide continued, oblivious to his spellbound students. Imitating the woman's voice and waving his hands in the air, he said, 'Oh, my. Oh, no. We have a problem!' "She wasn't sure how she was going to break the news to her guests that the mushrooms were poisonous." He chuckled to himself, and I couldn't understand what was funny. 'I'm afraid we're going to have to go to the emergency room and have our stomachs pumped,' she said. 'I fed some of the mushrooms to my husband's dog. The maid came and told me he's dead. Let's go. Now! I'm so sorry.'

I looked around at his fully captivated audience. He wasn't finished. "Just then, there was a knock on the hostess's front door. When she answered, standing before her was a middle-aged man with a pathetic look on his face. He said, 'I'm so sorry about your dog. I tried to swerve the car, but he ran out right in front of me. I took him to the vet hospital, but it was too late. He was killed instantly. Is there anything I can do?'

Our group of mushroom hunters began holding their stomachs and snorting out their noses with wild laughter. I smiled to cover up the look of terror on my face. This experience—true or not—not only ended that wealthy woman's mushroom hunting desire, but it also ended mine, too.

Don't French with a Wrench

I was heading home from Mankato, Minnesota, for Christmas break with my roommate, Penny, in my 1966 Toronado I'd recently purchased from my brother, Steve. I got a deal as he had lost my green 1964 Valiant when he failed to put a brick behind the back wheel. It rolled into a pond, and that was the end of it. I kept the brick in the trunk, along with an extra screwdriver to shift the gears in case the actual gear shift broke. What could I expect when the Valiant cost $60? The Toronado was definitely an upgrade.

We were about halfway home when I realized the car was drifting to the left. I wasn't sure whether snow on the road was causing the problem, or if it was something else. So, I pulled over on a dirt drive that led to a corn field.

"What're you doing?" Penny asked.

"The car isn't driving right. I have to check something."

I got out of the car, and saw that the rear tire on the driver's side was flat. I don't know how long I had driven on it, but it was basically shredded.

"I have a flat tire," I said, "you have to get out of the car."

"It's colder than a witch's tit out there."

"Well, stay in the car and pray it doesn't roll down the hill into that corn field," I said. "I hope you'll live through it. The car may roll side to side or maybe end to end."

"Okay. Okay!" Penny snapped. "What're we going to do?"

"No problem. I know how to change a tire. Didn't you take driver's training from Milo Hoel?"

"Yes, but I've never changed a tire. Do you have the right stuff to change it?"

"Not sure. This was my brother's car. If everything we need is in the trunk, we'll be a-okay." I hopped back into the car and engaged the parking brake. Opening the door, I shivered as the cold wind was overpowering. The snow was blowing and drifting, which would make changing the tire more difficult. We were on a Minnesota country road with no gas station, phone booth, or car in sight.

Penny watched as I opened the trunk. "Great! A spare," I said, as I pulled it out and bounced it a couple of times on the ground. It appeared to be full of air. Then I searched the trunk for a wrench. When I finally found it, I handed it to Penny.

"Hang on to this and I'll let you know when I need it."

"Can I sit in the car until you need it? I'm freezing."

"Do I need to explain again why you can't sit in the car?"

"Okay. I'll just shake and shiver."

"Sounds like rock and roll to me," I said, doing a mockup of the twist.

I pieced together the car jack and dug the snow out from under the car until I hit solid ground. I inserted the handle into the jack and placed it under the car frame. Carefully, I pumped the handle until the jack was secure and ready to raise the car.

I asked Penny for the wrench so I could loosen the lug nuts before raising the car. While she was handing it to me, it fell in the snow. I did the best I could to get the snow out of the end of the wrench, but when I tried to put it on the lug nut, it was still packed with too much snow for it to catch.

"Crap. The wrench is still packed with snow. We need to get it out so it'll work," I said.

"I'll look to see if I have something in my purse to dig it out," Penny said as she leaned into the front seat of the car.

I was trying to dig the snow out with my index finger, but it was so cold out that I couldn't leave my gloves off for very long. I became impatient waiting for Penny, so I stuck my tongue inside the wrench to melt the snow.

Bad idea! My tongue was instantly glued to the inside of the wrench.

When Penny came around the corner of the car and saw me with a wrench hanging from my mouth, she gave me the strangest look. "What are you doing?" she asked.

"My tongue is thuck," I said, as clearly as I could.

"Oh no. You've got to be kidding." She started laughing.

"Do I yook yike I'm kidding?" I said, trying to wiggle my tongue tip.

"Don't French with a wrench!" She paused and then began laughing so hard she fell over in the snow. "I can't believe I came up with that. Don't French with a wrench."

"Not funny. Help me. Thith hurtth," I said.

She came up closer to get a better look, but when our eyes met, we both broke into gut-wrenching laughter. We finally composed ourselves. At least the laughter warmed us up a bit.

"Is it really stuck or are you fooling me?" Penny asked.

"You think I'd have a wrenth on my tongue for the heck of it? Help!"

"Okay, okay," Penny said, trying to hold back her laughter.

"Weewee not funny. Get thith off my tongue," I yelled. "I can't thange the tire wike thith."

"Oh ya, that's a problem. Oh my . . . okay," I could tell that Penny was trying to come up with a plan. All I could think about was the wrench on the end of my tongue.

"I think I have a Coca Cola in my bag in the car. Maybe we can soak your tongue in that," she said.

She found the Coke and dribbled it on my tongue. It worked. My tongue tip was sore, but I was glad to be able to close my mouth. My teeth were freezing and the inside of my mouth was dry. I took a swig of Coke, then said, "We'll have to contact Coca Cola and tell them why everyone should have a can of Coke in their car if they live in Minnesota. You know this stuff originally contained cocaine. Wish it still did. My tongue wouldn't be so sore."

"I can't believe you did that."

"Shut up. You were taking too long to find something to dig out the snow. It's damn cold out here."

"You don't have to remind me. I'm now an ice sculpture."

I changed the tire as quickly as I could, and we were soon back on the road and heading to Blooming Prairie. My tongue was sore, but we had a good laugh, so I felt the whole ordeal was worth it.

Now, I have a AAA card, and I call THEM if I have a flat tire. Never again will I French with a wrench.

Speech, Roosters, and One Lucky Orphan

After I completed the first two years of college, I was accepted into the Speech and Language department at Mankato State College. I had excellent training with Doctors Brooks, Bernthal, and Beukelman—and Mrs. Kuster. She was not just my teacher. I babysat for her, too, and had fun playing with her kids and pretending to be a part of the family. My dad passed away before my senior year in college, and shortly thereafter, my mom met a mystic from India to whom she was devoted for sixteen years. That's another story, so I'll just say that the speech department became my extended family.

The classes were difficult, but I was determined to learn physics and anatomy. My first class was Introduction to Speech Pathology. Before my father, who had a laryngectomy, died, I interviewed him so the class could hear the sound of an electric larynx.

At the end of my first semester of my senior year, Dr. Beukelman required the class to write a paper on any disorder in Speech Pathology. I chose the effects of a laryngectomy. My dad was a smoker and had developed throat cancer when

I was a junior in high school. I attended his speech therapy classes with him at the Mayo Clinic in Rochester, Minnesota. That's when I decided to become a speech therapist. My dad wasn't able to accomplish esophageal speech, but he became proficient at the electric larynx. I shared his experience, in addition to facts and statistics about laryngectomies. I felt I was guaranteed to get a top grade.

When our papers were handed back, Dr. Beukelman didn't give me mine. He whispered that he wanted to see me after class. I assumed that he'd given me an A plus and that he didn't want any other students to feel badly. I met him in his office.

"Hello, Miss Thorson. I want to talk to you about your paper," he said as he handed it to me.

At the top was a D plus. I could feel my eyes welling up with tears and a lump starting in my throat.

"Miss Thorson. I want you to look at your first page. You start your sentence at the top and you finish it at the bottom. Do you see anything wrong with it?"

"No," I managed to squeak out.

"You write a sentence and then you add, 'and then' and go on to the next sentence. There is no punctuation. Did you write papers in English class at your high school?"

"Not much. We mostly worked on diagramming sentences." I began to cry.

"I liked your content and I've arranged for you to go to a remedial writing class. If you rewrite this paper, I'll regrade it. I'll have to give you a grade lower to be fair, but I'm willing to do that. Like you, I went to a small high school and I struggled with my college course work, but I was determined to succeed and you will, too."

"I feel so dumb," I said as he handed me a Kleenex.

"You aren't dumb, you just haven't been taught. Are you willing to take the remedial class?"

"Yes, I guess so."

He handed me the paper and assured me that I would be a great therapist and not to give up.

I took the class and returned my paper at the end of the two-week course. He graded it and handed it back to me. "I gave you a B because that was the fair thing to do. That means the paper was worth an A." I've never forgotten that experience and I never will.

My second semester I took a class with Dr. Brooks. He was older than my other professors and in charge of the program. I had him for clinical therapy; a class where you actually work with clients and learn what it takes to be a therapist. Hands-on training.

I started working with four-year-old, twin boys, Tommy and Johnny, on language acquisition. Tommy was more outspoken and developmentally farther along than Johnny, who learned early on to copy whatever Tommy said. They studied farm animals' names, the sounds they made, and what they did on the farm.

After a month, Dr. Brooks came in to observe me. It was test time for the kids. My hands were sweating, which smudged the paper on which I would record the boys' remarks. The plastic farm animals were lined up on the table, and the boys were sitting across from me. Dr. Brooks sat immediately behind me. I glanced back and he was busy marking a critique sheet for my grade. This increased my anxiety.

I would record the accuracy of the boys' answers by applying a gold star for each correct response. Having practiced this skill with the boys three times a week, it gave me confidence, but I knew I had to downplay Tommy's exuberance and Johnny's reluctance to participate.

"Okay, boys, we're going to play with our farm animals again today. I will give you a gold star on this special sheet every time you answer one of my questions. When we're done, you get to pick something out of the prize bucket."

"Prize now!" Tommy said. Johnny got up from his chair and went straight to the prize bucket.

"Johnny, sit down, please. Boys. Remember. Answer question. Gold star. Then prize," I said, realizing that trying to keep both boys on track was like herding cats. I heard a chuckle out of Dr. Brooks. I hoped that was a good thing. "Let's start the game so you can win the prize."

"Tommy, what is this animal?" I asked as I held a small white chicken in front of him.

"Chicken? Yes, chicken!" He flapped his arms as if he were a chicken. Johnny was giggling and started flapping his arms, also.

"Okay, Tommy, good job, but I have more questions. Here's a gold star for your sheet. Now, what does the chicken say?"

"Cluck, cluck," he said as he continued to flap his arms.

"Great. Here's another star. What does a chicken do?"

"Ummmm, eggs."

"Say the whole sentence. Chickens . . ."

"Chickens lay eggs."

"Yes, Tommy. Great job. Another star. Okay, Johnny. What is this animal?" I asked, as I held up a rooster.

"Chicken," he said. Johnny would copy whatever Tommy said if he didn't know the answer. He started flapping his arms just like Tommy.

"Yes, but we have another name for him. Remember? He's the daddy chicken. I'll give you a hint. He's a roo . . . roo," I said, giving him the beginning sounds of the word.

"Rooster," he said, flapping his arms again.

"Yes, here's your gold star. What does the rooster say?"

"Cluck, cluck," he said, remembering Tommy's answer with arms still flapping.

"That's what the mommy chicken says. Remember? What does the daddy chicken say?"

Tommy piped up. "Er- Er- Er!" He jumped out of his chair and started crowing.

"Tommy, it isn't your turn. Please, sit down. Johnny, let's try again. I want you to get your gold star. I'll give you a hint." I started the beginning of the word I wanted, which was cock-a-doodle-doo.

"Cock . . . cock." I realized what I was saying and Dr. Brooks was right behind me. I felt my face starting to flush. I quickly added, "Cock-a-doodle-doo. Remember? Repeat it after me."

"Cock-a-doo-doo," Johnny said as he flapped his arms again.

"Close enough. Good job. Here's your star. Now what does the rooster do early in the morning?" I asked, physically raising my chin and rounding my lips as a prompt for him to jump up and crow out loud, acting as if he was waking everybody up in the morning. We had practiced these many times.

"Roosters . . . roosters . . . roosters lay hens," Johnny said. He'd copied Tommy's verb and, somehow, he had remembered the word hen, but he had no idea the meaning of his sentence. He flapped his arms with the biggest grin on his face.

I froze. I didn't know what to do. I was sure my face was beet red.

Dr. Brooks leaned over and whispered in my ear, "Give him two stars for that answer."

***

Dr. Brooks not only had a sense of humor, but he also stepped up to the plate when I needed help. My mother went to India with her mystic right after I went back to college. Not long after, I was contacted by the university registrar's office. "Miss Thorson, I'm afraid your semester hasn't been paid for. You have a grace period of ten days."

"There must be a mistake. My mother is in India. I can send a Western Union telegram, but I think it will take more than ten days."

"Sorry, we have to follow policy. You won't be able to continue your classes."

I went directly to Dr. Brook's office. "I'm dropping out of the program," I said. "My mother is in India and she didn't pay for my final semester. I'm sorry. She hasn't been the same since my dad died." I started to cry. "I feel like an orphan."

"Now, now. I'm sure it's an oversight," he said, handing me a Kleenex.

"No, I thought about it. The mystic doesn't think a girl needs an education. He told me I should just find a good husband rather than going to school. He must have talked my mom out of paying my tuition."

"I want you to go to your apartment and write a couple of pages about why you think you would be a good therapist. I'll talk to the registrar's office to give us a little more time."

"Okay, but I think I better go to the student union to see if I can wash dishes or clean toilets."

"Just wait on that and bring me the paper tomorrow."

I went to the house I shared with my roommates and wrote the paper while wiping tears from my face. I didn't want anyone to know what had happened. I was embarrassed.

I returned the next day and gave the paper to Dr. Brooks. I figured he wanted me to write down my aspiration of becoming a speech therapist, so that someday I would come back and finish my course work.

"This is great. I want you to come to my Rotary Club meeting and read this paper to the group. I've made a few corrections, but very few."

I went with him to the meeting and met some wonderful people from the community. The next day, Dr. Brooks called me to his office. I knew he was going to ask me to clean out my locker and wanted to wish me luck. I was grateful for the writing task and decided I would get a job and save my money so I could come back.

"I want to congratulate you on your scholarship from the Rotary Club," he said. "They paid for your tuition and books, and here is a thousand-dollar check for your living expenses. Good job."

I was speechless. I began to cry, but these were tears of joy. Not only was I able to finish my degree, but I also learned a very valuable lesson—the wonderful model of giving back to those who need it when you yourself have made it.

My roommate, Vicki, lived in St. Paul and her family offered me a room for five months at no cost, while I completed my student teaching at local public schools and my clinical work at the Veterans Hospital. I was so blessed and filled with gratitude that I was able to complete my education and graduate.

That wasn't the end of the story, though. Forty years later, out of nowhere, I received a package from Mrs. Kuster and inside was a cassette tape. For a class project, I had recorded my father describing his experience having had a laryngectomy. As I listened to the tape, it brought back wonderful memories. Mrs. Kuster included a note congratulating me for having written the child development program, *My Baby Compass*. It warmed my heart. With teachers like mine, my success was inevitable.

Traveling in India

Tripping My Way Through

During the first semester of my senior year in college, my mother invited me and my younger brother, Ronny, to come visit and get to know her mystic in Prasanth, India. My professors at Mankato State allowed me to leave a month early and I was required to write a term paper for independent study.

I had a stopover in England, and waited for my brother to arrive and accompany me for the rest of the trip. As I was waiting for him, I stayed with a friend of my mother's named Brenda. She was in her forties and was always formally dressed, a prim and proper English woman. It was the early seventies and I was all about halter tops, bell bottoms, frayed jeans, free love and peace signs. I was so excited to be in the same country as The Beatles.

Brenda was the headmaster at a private girl's school and was gone during the day. She had very definite ideas about what I should do while she was gone, starting with Hampton Court Palace, which was near where she lived. "I don't want you screwed into the telly all day. There are many fine things to see here in London."

I laughed. "Screwed into what?"

"The idiot box. The television," she said sharply. She was a persnickety spinster, and I realized I had better toe the line.

"I made you a soft-boiled egg with some prosciutto and British tea. I will be back in the early afternoon," she said.

She brought me the egg in an egg cup. I had never seen an egg presented in this manner. I figured it was hard-boiled and needed peeling, so I took it out of the cup. It hadn't been cooked long enough and it fell apart. Egg yolk dripped all over my hands.

Just then, Brenda came back into the kitchen to get her car keys. "My, oh my. What a mess. What are you doing? Use your spoon!" she said, her large frame towering over me.

"I've never seen an egg in a cup like this. I thought I was supposed to peel it. What is this next to it? It looks like colored cellophane."

"You Americans have no class. It's prosciutto. It's a fine salami. I will make you another egg and I'll show you how to eat it. Have you never seen an egg cup?"

"Nope. Not even at the Cozy Inn Restaurant in Blooming Prairie."

"Why am I not surprised?" She rolled her eyes and took my mess back to the kitchen.

She came back with another egg in the egg cup. She showed me how to tap the egg at the top, remove the tip of the eggshell and sprinkle salt and pepper.

"Do you have some ketchup?" I asked.

"Did you say ketchup? You aren't going to put that on your egg?"

"A . . . yah. That's how you eat eggs in Minnesota. With ketchup."

"Not here. I don't even have ketchup. It's just old tomatoes with a lot of sugar. Not good for you and it kills the taste of your food. You will learn to eat your egg without ketchup while you are living at my flat," she said, with special emphasis on *you will learn*.

"What's a flat?" I asked. "Isn't that something that happens to your tires?"

"It means my apartment."

"I don't think they have flats in Blooming Prairie. Never heard of one anyway."

"I don't think you've heard of much," she said with a look of disgust as she went out the door for work.

"I'll try the egg without the ketchup," I yelled.

I tried to get my spoon inside the egg. The hole wasn't large enough. I then tapped on the egg a little lower. The edge of the spoon went through the egg and chunks of egg and shell went flying across the room. I used my dainty cloth napkin to pick up the mess. I flushed it down the toilet and washed out the cloth napkin.

Now I had only a half egg. I took my spoon and flipped the egg out of the shell. It splatted on the saucer next to the meat that was still a big question mark in my mind. It looked somewhat like bologna, but it had white streaks and you could see right through it. I mixed the egg with the meat and ate it. I missed the ketchup, but I wouldn't starve.

I peered into the fine china cup. It appeared to hold a light-colored cocoa, but when I sipped it, I discovered it wasn't cocoa, but some type of tea with milk. I spit it out and dumped the rest in the sink. I then washed the evidence off my china plate so Brenda wouldn't find out that I didn't use the egg cup.

When I went out to explore, I was still hungry due to my breakfast fiasco. I was a swimmer and was used to a healthy diet. I stopped at a cute café with outdoor seating and ordered a hamburger and French fries. When my food arrived, the waiter took a bottle and sprinkled what I thought was water on my fries.

"I can let my French Fries cool. You don't have to sprinkle water on them," I said.

"That's vinegar, not water."

"Excuse me, sir," I said, "but I don't like vinegar on my French fries. I want ketchup."

There was silence as all the customers turned and stared at me. The waiter picked up my vinegar-soaked French fries. "I'm sorry. We have no ketchup. I'll bring you back more French fries."

I could tell he, like Brenda, was a little disgusted, but I really couldn't fathom eating my fries with vinegar. I didn't eat anything with vinegar—that was something my mom made me swallow if I was sick. I ate the second order of French Fries, but I missed the ketchup. Then I followed Brenda's instructions and visited Hampton Court Palace before heading back to the 'flat.'

The first thing Brenda asked when she came home was how my day went. I wasn't about to mention the French Fries incident, but I was happy to tell her I'd gone to

Hampton Court. "I learned about Henry VIII, his wives and children at Tudor court. He wasn't a very good husband, in my opinion. He cut off a couple of heads of his wives. Maybe they didn't know how to use an egg cup either," I said, hoping Brenda would find it funny. She didn't. I added, "The Haunted Gallery was creepy, but the rest of the place was beautiful. I loved the gardens."

"I'm glad you are taking in some history and beauty. Tomorrow you should take a trip on the subway and go into town. I think you would find more to do." She gave me a subway map and directions to the entryway.

"What time do you want me to knock you up in the morning?" Brenda asked.

"What did you say?" I was laughing so hard I could hardly get the words out.

"The time you want to rise."

I could tell she wasn't used to having a younger person living with her and making fun of her word choices.

"Whatever is good for you. I'm just winging it," I said.

"What is winging it?"

"Going with the flow."

"And that is?"

"It means I have no plans. I'm unscheduled."

"Doesn't sound like a productive visit to me." I could tell we were made from two different types of cloth. She was a starched cotton petticoat and I was more well-worn jeans with holes.

"I'm having a great time and I appreciate your letting me stay here until my brother arrives," I said, knowing I would gain more with honey than vinegar. I knew there was a reason I didn't like vinegar.

The next day, I followed Brenda's instructions and took the bus to the subway. There were people playing music with their guitar cases open for tips, posters announcing theatre performances, people selling watches and jewelry from the inside of their long coats and the loud roar of the subway trains flying by. A much different experience from downtown Blooming Prairie, which didn't even have a stoplight.

I was on my way to Buckingham Palace. I had never seen a queen before. The closest I came was naming my dog, Princess. I smiled as I remembered how I told my dad that Princess was a natural born leader, when really, the other dogs were following her because she was in heat.

When I arrived at the palace, they were in the middle of the changing of the guard. It was a very formal production and people were gathered around taking pictures. The guards showed no expression. I guess I wouldn't either if I had to do that job. Standing there all day with nothing to do, but hold your gun. Who was going to steal the Queen anyway?

I approached a person I'd overheard who spoke with a British accent. "When do we get to see the Queen?" I asked. "I came all the way from America to see her."

He laughed. "She isn't scheduled for an appearance today."

"I heard she rides her horses and stuff. Will I get to see her if I visit her stables?" I had been in love with horses since I was a little girl.

"You can buy a ticket to tour the stables, but you won't see the queen," he said.

I was disappointed, but I bought the ticket. The carriages were elegant and a coachman who worked for the queen talked about how each was used and when. The Queen had a barn full of horses. They were beautifully groomed and attendants removed every speck of manure as soon as the horses left any in their stalls. That wouldn't happen at home in my small town, because pasture barns were cleaned out twice a year with a Bobcat. Seeing the stables was an exciting experience for me, even without the Queen.

"How was your day today?" Benda asked when I got back to the flat.

"I had a great time. I went to Buckingham Palace to see the Queen, but that didn't happen. I guess I have to get used to 'no Queen' and 'no ketchup.'"

"I think there is more for you to get used to, but your brother is going to be here very soon, so you will have to come visit me again," she said with a forced smile. I don't think she really meant it, but I smiled back with the same forced expression.

There probably won't be ketchup in India either, but at least Brenda wouldn't be there to force me to eat eggs out of an egg cup.

Don't Drink the Juice

When Ronny and I arrived in Mangalore, India, the closest airport to Prasanth, our older brother Ty was there to meet us. Ty and Mom had been in India for a month before Ronny and I joined them, so Ty knew the ropes. He hailed a taxi to take us to the train station. Ronny and I were surprised that, in India, a taxi is a bicycle toting a cart with one seat. The cart barely had enough room for the three of us. We placed our luggage on our laps. It was a good thing we were young, thin, and had packed light. I felt sorry for the Indian man that was using all of his strength to pull us.

"What's the mystic's place like?" I asked Ty.

"It's gorgeous. It's in the middle of a jungle in southern India and it's a coconut and cashew plantation. We have to look out for the cobras, scorpions, and tigers," Ty said, with a laugh.

"What! You've got to be kidding." Blooming Prairie, Minnesota, has NO poisonous anything. I was in culture shock.

"What happens if we get bitten or attacked?" I asked.

"You die," Ty said, laughing again. "It's alright. You have to stay on the elevated paths and sweep out your shoes for scorpions before you put them on. Also, look for critters in the makeshift bathroom, which is like an outhouse. And don't walk around at night."

"I can handle that. Good thing we have Ronny. We can use him as bait for the tigers."

"No way," Ronny said.

The streets in Mangalore were bustling with scooters, bicycles, bicycle taxis, and so many people. Women were wearing saris or burkas, and men wore lungis, a cloth that looks like a long, white skirt, and sometimes, it is tied around the waist and the bottom of the skirt is tucked into the waist to make baggy shorts. White is the predominate color. I soon learned why. It was hot! While riding in the bicycle taxi we had to avoid the cows freely walking in the streets. They were sacred—a far cry from the Black Angus at home.

"You know you won't be eating any meat accept fish. The family we're staying with is primarily vegetarian," Ty said.

"What's a vegetarian?" I asked.

"A person who doesn't eat meat."

"Like no hamburgers or hot dogs?" Ronny asked.

"Oh, my. We're going to starve!" I said.

"I think you'll like the food. They do eat duck eggs and milk from cows," Ty said.

"Duck eggs? I didn't know you could eat those. And they milk the cow and you drink the milk right away? It isn't pasteurized" I asked.

"Yes, you drink the milk right away. There isn't any refrigeration. They grow all their own food except they barter with the fish lady that comes every day to the farm. She carries a large basket on her head and it's full of the catch of the day," Ty said.

"Okay. This is going to be an adventure," I said. "Sorry, Ronny. I don't think they have macaroni and cheese or canned cherries." Ty and I laughed.

We bought our tickets, and as we waited for our train, I saw a small sidewalk food cart selling sugar cane juice. I was thirsty and I talked my two brothers into buying some. The man running the cart handed us a glass. One glass, that was all he had. Ronny and I drank most of it, with Ty taking only a sip. I stopped when I saw the dead fly at the bottom of the glass. I gagged and was so grossed out that I wasn't thirsty anymore.

We got on the train for Prasanth, the cashew and coconut plantation where we were staying. When we arrived, we were greeted by Amma and Appa, the couple who owned the plantation. They were the parents of Shri Krishnaji, my mother's mystic.

At four o'clock, we had tea. I soon learned that teatime was a daily ritual when guests would visit and we would be entertained by snake charmers or young children who could sing or dance. The tea was hot, made British style with milk and sugar, and served with biscuits, which were actually shortbread cookies.

That first afternoon, we met some guests with important positions in the Indian company Tata. The guests wanted to speak English. However, they said "Goodbye" when they met us, and when they left, they said, "Hello." It was all I could do to keep my composure so I didn't embarrass them. After they left, Ty, Ronny, and I sang the Beatles' song "Hello, Goodbye" together and laughed our heads off as our mother shook her head at our silliness and smiled.

We were settling into our thatched-roof hut before supper at the main house when my stomach started churning. The next thing I knew, Ronny and I were both sick. Then Ty joined us. We were tossing our cookies in the bathroom, which was a hole in the ground surrounded by woven, upright palm leaves secured by bamboo. There was a bucket of water to clean ourselves, but no sink, no electricity, no toilet paper, or paper towels. Ty reminded us to keep a close watch for the scorpions, which was hard to do when your stomach was rumbling!

My poor mother wasn't prepared for this. We didn't have any Lomotil, Imodium, or anything like that. We didn't even have aspirin. This was my introduction to India. Not a great way to start.

Our dysentery continued, and it was so severe that we began to get weak. Ty, Ronny, and I spent much of our time lying on our small cots. My mother had to wash out our clothes by hand. She hung the wet clothes on tree limbs, palm leaves, and window ledges. She was running out of room and we were running out of clothes to wear. My younger brother was in the most distress because he was only fifteen years old and skinny for his age. He didn't need to lose any weight. After a couple of weeks, we weren't any better and my mother asked for a doctor to come to the plantation. The doctor had to travel hours in a small, motorized car that looked like a souped-up golf cart.

The doctor entered the three-room hut and greeted us with a smile because he didn't speak English. Then he pulled out the largest syringe I'd ever seen. It looked like the syringes we used on the farm pigs in Blooming Prairie. He inserted a needle in my arm and proceeded to fill me with fluid. I think it was some type of hydrating IV drip administered straight from the syringe. It was all I could do not to faint. I don't do well with needles and blood.

"You're next," I called to my brothers. "This stuff he brought us to drink tastes like chalk. The bottle's labeled Lemon Sludge. I think the beverage bottle was rinsed out and this concoction was poured into it. They need to rethink that name for marketing purposes. It would never make it in the U.S."

The doctor performed the same procedure on each of my brothers. I could hear their groans. I wasn't so sure that the doctor changed the needle.

We lay there for days, and our mother spent a lot of time with us. Once we started feeling a little better, the jokes and stories kept coming. We would dream about what we would have for breakfast, lunch, and dinner, and talk about it.

"Do you guys realize that tomorrow is Thanksgiving? I wonder how they celebrate it in India," I said.

"They don't celebrate Thanksgiving. That's a pilgrim thing. It's American," Ty informed me.

"Wow, are they missing out. Turkey, mashed potatoes, sweet potatoes, peas, cranberry cake with butter sauce. And

Mom's caramel rolls. Mom, can you make your sticky buns here in Prasanth?" I asked.

"Don't say sticky buns. I already have those," Ronny said.

Ty and I started laughing. We needed it. At the time, laughter really was the best medicine.

"No, I can't bake sticky buns in their oven," Mom said. "They use wood and there is no electricity or the right ingredients to make the rolls. A food for you to look forward to when you are back home."

"So, we're going to have Lemon Sludge for Thanksgiving?"

"It looks that way. Maybe I can have Amma make some chapatis," Mom said, trying to make lemonade out of Lemon Sludge.

Remembering our first teatime, I started to sing "Hello, Goodbye" and Ronny and Ty began to laugh. It was good to see Mom laughing along with us, since she was taking care of the three of us. It was hard work for her, and she was supposed to be on vacation.

"How about the fact that they don't think anything about farting in front of us?" Ronny said.

We laughed again. We were desperate and even bathroom humor was funny.

When Thanksgiving arrived and we were still sucking down Lemon Sludge, I imagined that each swig was a taste of Mom's Thanksgiving dinner. We managed to make it through that deadly experience and I learned not eat anything off the street in a new country. The bacteria are different and our bodies do not have a natural immunity. It made me appreciate the boiled water and food that Amma made sure was properly prepared for our American stomachs.

I don't know if it was the fact that I hadn't had solids for so long, but my taste for food changed. I actually kicked the ketchup habit. I learned to like Indian spices: cardamom, turmeric, cumin, nutmeg, cloves, vanilla, and cinnamon, besides the various curries. I loved everything that was baked in the wood-fired oven, but my favorite was naan, an unleavened bread. Sometimes Amma would brush it with ghee, which is clarified butter, and sprinkle crushed garlic that was just picked from the garden.

I watched how hard the servants worked. They each had their duties throughout the day. Most of them had worked for Amma and Appa for years. As I walked through the garden on the elevated paths, I could see pepper on the vines, cinnamon in its virgin form, mangoes, papayas, jackfruit, and plantains, which are like small bananas. The plantation was a paradise full of fresh fruit, spices, coconut milk, rice, eggs, cow's milk, ghee, and cashew nuts.

I learned to eat healthier. Pizza, burgers, fried foods and sugared cereals became a thing of the past. I didn't need to go to a health spa or read books by doctors. I learned from the master, a woman in her eighties, who lived in India. Her name was Amma.

Misfit on Ooty Tea Plantation

While I was in India, and awaiting my return to my last semester in college, my mother and I traveled with Baba Shri Kishnaji to the Ooty Tea Plantation, which was in the Blue Mountains. We toured the 800-plus acres, learned about the production of the tea, and tasted their rare and valuable Nilgiri tea. This is a full-bodied brew that resembles Ceylon teas and received its name from the location where it's produced—Nilgiri actually means "Blue Mountain." The best harvests occur from January to March, and we were lucky to see one.

We were guests of the Maharaja of Mysore, an important Indian dignitary under British rule, because my mother was in the process of developing a business relationship with India and setting up a corporation. I had been in India for a couple of months by this time and was missing interaction with people my own age. Especially boys.

The owners of the tea estate treated us like royalty. When we arrived, we were served cups of tea. The Indians prepare hot tea differently than we do in the United States. The water is boiled, poured over the tea leaves, and steeped for exactly three minutes. Any longer, and it becomes bitter. Then, milk and sugar are heated separately so the milk doesn't scald, and the brewed tea is added.

I developed a taste for tea and I enjoyed the daily tea-time at four-o-clock, which was the time of day that guests would arrive and share stories or entertainment. As I was sipping my tea, I noticed a young man who appeared to be my age. He was very handsome and well dressed. I walked over to him.

"Hi, my name is Kathy," I said with a sweet smile.

He nodded, smiled and quickly looked down at the floor. Shy, I thought. Shyness wasn't my problem. I could talk for both of us.

"It's beautiful here. I'm in college in the United States. How about you?"

He smiled again and looked down at the floor.

I persisted. "This is a great cup of tea. I'm sure you drink it all the time. We don't drink tea like this in the states. It's usually in a tea bag."

He nodded again and continued to look at the floor.

Boy, was he playing hard to get! I was even more determined to get him to talk to me.

"I play the guitar. Do you like music?" I asked, as I bent over to make eye contact, my long hair almost touching the floor, and my face only inches away from his. He had the most beautiful eyes.

"Excuse me!" I heard a deep voice say.

I looked up and saw a man dressed in a military uniform. He was wearing a turban. He looked angry.

"Hi, my name—"

He didn't let me finish my introduction. "I don't need to know your name. My son is betrothed and he isn't able to talk to you."

"Sorry. Is betrothed a disease and that's why he can't talk?"

I heard laughter from a few old men that were sitting at a table drinking their tea. I'd never heard the word 'betrothed.'

"His marriage has already been arranged. That is betrothed. It is our custom in our country. I have already received the dowry from the bride's family."

"What's a dowry?" I asked.

"In our country, marriages are arranged. My wife and I have chosen five women that would be appropriate and he has chosen one. The bride's family is responsible for providing a dowry. A dowry is either money or property that is worthy of my son. The bride's family is very wealthy and we are receiving a large dowry. It will be a magnificent wedding."

"Holy crap!" I said.

"What is crap? I don't know that word," he said.

"No, you misunderstood. I said 'hat.'" I couldn't explain a not-very-polite slang word that just flew out of my mouth to such a dignified man. I was just so shocked to learn that a marriage was something that could be arranged. "I was saying that your son must have to wear a holy hat for his wedding. Kind of like your hat. Right?"

"It's a turban. The wedding is holy. We are Hindu. How old are you?"

"I'm twenty."

"You aren't married?"

"Hell no!" I said quickly.

"Did you say 'hell'?" he asked in a stern manner.

"No, I said 'hello.' My dialect must be confusing," I said, thinking I better cross my fingers behind my back and get out of this conversation.

"You are an old woman. You better find a man soon and get married."

"I have plenty of time. I'm in college and I want to finish my degree."

"You chose a career over a husband?" he said.

"No, I'll probably get married someday."

"That can't happen here. A woman must choose whether she wants a career or a husband. It is our custom," he said. "Now you must be on your way and not talk to my son."

"No problem. I hope you'll enjoy the wedding."

I was in shock. *A career or a husband?* Well, if I lived in India, it would definitely be a career. If my dad were still alive, he was cheap and there was no way he would have paid any guy to marry me. I would've ended up with the town drunk!

"Kathryn, we are going to take a tour of the tea plantation. Please be our guest," a nicely dressed servant said to me as he approached me, my mother, and Baba Shri Krishnaji. The servant continued, "I talked to the Maharaja of Mysore and he is willing to give you the tiger skin that you were admiring."

"Wow. That'll look great in my bedroom. I've never seen one before," I said.

The next thing I knew, Baba Shri Krishnaji, who had taken a vow of silence, appeared to be on the verge of talking for the first time in twenty-two years. He grunted loudly and the woman who accompanied him interpreted his hand signals and said, "That won't be necessary. No gifts."

My mother gave me a dirty look and we headed for the area where the tea is harvested on the estate. I was feeling pretty fed up. I didn't need to talk to any boys or receive a tiger rug, I was looking forward to learning how tea was produced, anyway. I later learned that, in India, when it comes to business, gifts aren't free, and that the rug was a real tiger skin. They are endangered species and I would have felt awful knowing a tiger had been killed on my behalf.

I found the tea process fascinating, which took my mind off boys and tiger rugs. After the leaves have been plucked, the real tea production begins. Before they leave the tea factory, all the teas—black, green, white, and oolong—are graded and sorted. Because different-sized leaves brew at different speeds, the leaves are separated into batches of the same size. We were told that the smaller the leaf, the more valuable the tea.

The tea leaves go through four stages. The first stage, withering, is when the tea leaves are laid out in big wire mesh trays to reduce the water content to about 65 percent. Then, the rolling stage twists and turns the leaves until they are thin and wiry looking. The oxidation process, which determines the tea's color, taste and strength, changes the leaves' color from greenish beige to a rich, deep brown by exposing the tea to a temperature of about 78 degrees Fahrenheit for between thirty minutes and two hours. The last stage, drying in hot air dryers, further reduces their water content to about three percent, leaving the tea leaves ready to be sorted and packed.

I saw the men sweeping up and bagging the tea that had fallen on the floor. I was told they refer to it as American tea and is used in tea bags. I was hoping they were joking, but they weren't.

We were excited about the idea of importing these delicious tea leaves as a business and my mother looked into shipping it to the United States. She discovered that the shipping process is dominated by Lipton and Twinning and that the tea would have to be airlifted, making it far too expensive per pound.

This was a frustrating end to a trip that, with the exception of learning a lot about tea, had been pretty disappointing, at least for me. Oh, well. It sure made me appreciate how great it was to talk to boys and date whomever I wanted. And no tigers lost their lives for my sake.

Perilous Journey

In 1974, India and Pakistan were at war. Of course, to a family like ours from a small town in southern Minnesota, this didn't seem to matter. Why should this stop my mother, two brothers and me from traveling to India? We were visiting my mother's mystic, Shri Krishnaji, also known as Baba, but Mom was also looking to start a business importing an Indian product. We had consulted with 3M in Minnesota for possible imports, and were scouting for exports. The tea idea didn't work out, and so we investigated handwoven carpets, guar gum, and gems as possibilities. Baba was a spiritual leader to many government officials and, despite the vow of silence he'd taken years ago, had business contacts all over India and Europe.

We didn't understand all that was going on in India at this time. India and Russia had close ties because Russia was providing military support for India's conflict in Kashmir. The railway workers were threatening to strike, which encouraged many union workers to join them. India was also in the midst of a general political crisis and sections of the peasantry were revolting. There we were, in the middle of it all, not realizing what political consequences were lurking. We didn't feel threatened or in danger. However, as time went on, Mom's exploration of possible imports began to face mounting challenges. And so did our sightseeing arrangements.

We had originally planned to go to New Delhi, but the Russians were recruiting insurgents to march and hold rallies there. It wouldn't have been prudent for Americans to travel in an area with such political policies, especially since the United States was backing Pakistan. So, Baba encouraged us to skip New Delhi and come straight to his plantation in Prasanth, which was in southern India.

It was great fun spending time with family on his coconut and cashew plantation in the middle of a jungle. We played guitars, hiked to the top of the mountains, played chess, and read books. My mother and I also traveled to safe places in the remote countryside while we were chaperoned by Baba.

Everything about our trip worked out well despite the political upheaval—until I had to get back to the University of Minnesota, Mankato. I had overstayed my sabbatical due to the transportation strike in India, and I would lose credit for my independent study if I didn't leave immediately.

"If you don't get me out of here, I'll hitchhike!" I yelled at my mother, reverting back momentarily to a teenager from the Land of Gland.

"I was told it wasn't safe to travel to the airport," my mother calmly answered.

"I'll steal a bicycle. I did it before. I'll do it again. I'm not losing a semester of school. I have to sign up for my student teaching experience."

"You don't need an education. You're beautiful. You just need a good husband. We will find one for you," Baba wrote on a piece of paper and handed it to me.

"Really?" I started to laugh. "I've been running my own life since I was twelve. Do you really think I'm going to listen to some man? I'm not the marrying type. And if I do change my mind, I'll pick him out myself, thank you very much."

My mother turned to Baba and said, "My daughter is very independent. Are you sure there isn't some way to get her home?"

Baba rolled his eyes and shook his head. Then he looked up in the air and groaned. I could tell he was stressed. My mom and I quietly waited. Finally, he patted at the air with his hands, gave an OK sign and smiled, indicating that everything would be alright.

With Baba's guidance, my mother arranged to have my brother Ronny and me travel by private car to Bombay (now Mumbai) and catch a plane. It was a two-day drive. Due to the strikes, it was impossible to predict which areas might be facing opposition. So, Baba rented an additional car to ride ahead of ours. It carried four Indian men whose job it was to clear our path if protesters were in the way. Our Mercedes sedan held two Indian men in the front seat, and two others wedged into the back seat with my brother and myself. We were instructed to lie down on the floor immediately if we came upon a group of rioters. We would then be hidden under a small oriental rug, and the men would put their feet on top of it.

We were traveling overnight because Baba thought that was safest. Ronny and I were fast asleep in the back seat when I heard, "Get on the floor. Now!" One of the Indian men shook me awake and we threw ourselves down on the floor of the car. I could squish my five-foot-four frame on my side, but I still don't understand how Ronny, at six-foot-five, managed. As planned, the oriental rug was put on top of us and the men placed their feet gently on top.

I felt the car stop and heard screaming and sticks banging. Soon the whole car was shaking.

"Ronny, grab my hands," I said. Our heads were almost touching.

"Why?" he asked.

"I heard the men say that if the protesters flip the car, they're going to put their hands on the roof of the car, hold their feet against our backs, and not let anyone see us until the car in front can help."

"What does that mean?"

"I don't know. That's all I heard them say."

I started singing "Hello, Goodbye" in the softest voice I could. Ronnie and I needed something light and funny to think about. Just then, we heard men screaming and yelling and felt the car being lifted and then tipping.

Ronny and I hung on to each other. I felt the pressure of the Indian man's feet on my back.

Then I heard gunshots and the car suddenly dropped. There was a brief moment of silence.

"Holy crap," I whispered to Ronny.

My heart was beating wildly as our driver sped off. We heard more shouting and screaming as the car swerved from side to side. I don't know how long we were under the rug, but it seemed like forever.

The car eventually stopped. The two men in the back seat with us pulled back the rug.

"You can get up now and sit in the seat," one of them said.

"Okay," I said, looking around. From what I could see, we were in the middle of a dark forest. Because of the lack of electricity throughout the rural area, it was jet black except for the area illuminated by the car's headlights. It was so dark that I couldn't see the car that had been in front of us for our protection. We didn't ask any questions. We were too afraid. Before long, Ronny and I fell asleep again, our heads leaning against each other between the two men.

The next morning, bright sunlight filtered through the window and woke me up. The four men were talking in Malayalam, their Indian dialect. I had no idea what they were saying, but I suspected it was about what happened during the night.

"Do we have far to go? I need to potty," I said.

"We will stop soon. It is four more hours to the airport in Bombay," our driver said.

At the top of a curvy road, the car stopped. I realized that, in this case, 'the bathroom' was the biggest bush you could find to hide behind to do your deed. I walked to a bush that would cover me well. I didn't go far for fear of cobras, scorpions or any of the many other poisonous creatures that

I'd encountered at Prasanth. I had just crouched down and started to relieve myself when I heard gunshots. I fell over with my bottom in the air, just short of falling in the puddle I had made.

"Ahhhhh," I screamed, as I rolled on my back in the dirt, trying to pull up my pants.

The next thing I knew, one of the men was next to me. "You screamed. Are you okay?"

"I'm fine. I'm trying to go to the bathroom."

"Do women lay down to go to the bathroom in America?" he asked.

"No, we usually have a throne to sit on," I said sarcastically. "No bushes, no hole in the floor, no latrines. A real bathroom with a toilet. AND toilet paper," I said, getting up as I tried to wipe the dust off my pants. "And we can use our left hand for everything. We don't have to hide it on our lap under the kitchen table because we don't use a cup of water from the bucket and our left hand to wipe ourselves."

"Toilet paper is nasty. You don't clean yourself off with water?" he asked.

I started to think about what he said. Washing myself off with water was making sense. "We wash after the toilet paper," I said.

"With your left hand?" he asked.

I could tell this conversation was going in circles, so I changed the subject. "I heard gunshots."

"One of the men shot in the air to scare the baboons that were along the hillside. I guess one became aggressive when a man was trying to prepare some food for us. They didn't kill any of them, but it scared the bunch away. They can bite."

"I thought you couldn't have a gun in India?" I asked.

"They are military. Hired by the general at the request of your mother and Baba."

So, that's where the gunshots came from when our car was being tipped over and then suddenly let go.

The men gave us some bread, canned cheese, and bottled drinks. They offered us some type of curry, but I knew it would be so hot it would burn our mouths, and there was no yogurt to cool it off.

"I can't stand this cheese," I whispered to Ronny. "With all these cows walking around, you would think we could get some decent cheese."

"This isn't Minnesota or Wisconsin," Ronny said.

"That's for sure. Wow, that was some ride last night."

"And I'm sure you weren't supposed to sing a Beatles tune. We were hiding. Remember?"

"I was nervous. I had to lighten the moment. It worked, so shut up." A typical response from me, his big sister. "Do you want some more bread? It's naan."

"Naw."

"None. Naw. Naan." I laughed as I repeated the words, then got up and danced in place. I raised my arms and twirled, singing and laughing. I was glad to be alive.

The Indian men stopped talking and one looked at me. "You are such a silly girl," he said, as he shook his head from side to side.

"You betcha, by golly," I said, knowing he wouldn't understand Minnesota slang. I'm sure my behavior was much different from the young girls he knew.

I looked out over the peaceful hillside, and watched the workers in the field. I didn't ask about the riot or what happened, and the men didn't give us any information voluntarily.

The last few hours of our trip were uneventful. We arrived at the airport and boarded the plane with no incidents. Finally, it was time to relax.

Then, our plane made a stop in Tehran, Iran, for fuel on our way to Frankfurt, Germany, where we would catch our flight to New York. I looked out the window and saw that the plane was being circled by men in turbans and robes. Their chests were crisscrossed with leather straps holding rows of bullets. I thought the excitement was over when we left the car in Bombay. "Ronny!" I said, as I realized he was fast asleep.

Three men boarded the plane. One of them was talking to the stewardess and pilots as the other two came walking down the aisle. They were each looking side to side at the passengers.

"Don't look at them. Look at the floor," the man on the other side of me said.

"Why?" I asked quietly.

"Hush. Look at the floor," he whispered.

I was looking at the floor and I could see the sandals of one of the men who was checking out the passengers. He had stopped by my seat. Out of habit, I looked up. We made eye contact. He smiled, but it wasn't a smile that told me everything was alright. It was a mean smirk. I quickly looked down. I didn't have a good feeling. He stood there a little longer before he moved on. I was the only blonde, blue-eyed girl on the plane.

The next thing I knew, the three men left the plane and we were on our way. The man sitting next to me went up to the front of the plane. He returned to his seat.

"What was that all about?" I asked.

"The stewardess told me they were looking for spies."

"Were there spies on the plane?"

"One person left the plane. No one knows why. The pilots were then given permission to leave."

Could I have been taken off that plane and sold into slavery? I shivered at the thought. That smirk is vivid in my memory to this day. Western civilization was being challenged in Iran. The United States was backing the Shah of Iran as he westernized the country. There was fear among the religious leaders that their customs would be lost forever.

As soon as we get to America, I'm going to kiss the ground I walk on.

I made it home in time to report to my university and my independent study was accepted. I didn't tell my professors that I risked both my brother's life and my own. They would've never believed it. Sometimes, I still can't believe it!

Living Married in Rochester

Love in the Saddle

I think it's interesting how people meet their future husband or wife. It's a question I like to ask couples. For most, it's a memorable moment.

The first time I met my future husband, Bill, it was when he was dating my roommate, Jill. She had so many other men after her that Bill was just a number. He found out about the other guys and ended the relationship. I ran into Bill again a year later. Well, I actually didn't run into him. I was on my horse.

As I was riding by the Mayowood Stone Barn in Rochester, Minnesota, I saw a horse going in circles, completely out of control. I rode up to help and realized the rider was Bill. He looked like Little Joe Cartwright on the *Bonanza* television show. His deep-set eyes, dark curly hair, and cheeky grin reminded me of the crush I had on Little Joe when I was a young girl.

"Hi. Do you need help?" I asked.

"Yah, can I follow you so this horse will go straight? Trying to train him. Just bought him. He's turning three. Not very polished," he said as the horse made a 360-degree turn with each phrase he uttered.

"Was he that unruly when you tried him out?"

"Oh, I didn't try to ride him. I just bought him," he said, as he and the horse twirled around for the fifth time.

I walked my horse over next to his and let them sniff noses. His horse, Sian, was interested and started to follow my horse as I slowly walked toward the trail. We kept our pace to a walk as we made our way through the woods. Sian followed well. I believe the horse was as relieved as Bill.

"Is your name Bill?" I asked.

"Yes, how did you know?"

"I believe you dated my roommate, Jill. My name's Kathy."

"Jill, wow, that was a while ago. I'm not seeing her now. I thought she moved in with her boyfriend?"

"She moved to Washington state. I think she got married. Not sure. We aren't in touch anymore." I smiled to myself as I thought about my roommate Jill and her antics. We did have fun.

"What's your name again?" he asked.

"Kathy. Kathy Thorson to be exact." I would soon learn that names weren't Bill's forte.

We came to a junction in the trail. A two-foot log blocked the right fork. Bill rode up to the log and let Sian look at it.

"This horse can jump. Do you want to see?" Bill said.

Before I could say no—because the horse wasn't broken well enough to be jumping, and Bill clearly wasn't skilled enough to be schooling him—he trotted the horse about twenty feet back and headed for the jump.

About ten feet before the log, Sian took off at a dead run, jumped about four feet over the log, landed and ran into the woods, through vines and bramble. The horse was completely out of control. Both horse and rider were gone. The scene looked like something out of a cartoon. You could see the outline a horse and rider had left in the thick brush.

I waited, but Bill didn't show up. I waited longer. I started to get worried that he was hurt and unconscious somewhere in the woods. So, I walked my horse up the trail calling out his name. Soon Bill appeared, scratches on his face and neck. His jodhpurs were shredded. There were leaves stuck inside the bridle and a small branch with thorns was dragging from Sian's tail.

"Well, how was the jump?" Bill asked, with a big smile on his face.

I couldn't believe it. Bill almost met death, and he wanted me to critique his horse's ability to jump? He was crazy.

Well, that's when I knew I was going to marry him. Yep. Right then and there. A man that thought he could do anything. I liked that. And he looked like Little Joe, which was icing on the cake. After that, we went trail riding through Mayowood together on a regular basis. Our friendship grew.

A few months later, Bill invited me for dinner. Since he was a resident with a medical school loan, he told me that the only thing he could afford was the International House of Pancakes. I was a struggling first year teacher and said that was fine. We agreed on a time for him to pick me up, but it ended up being a quick dinner because he was on a cardiology rotation and was called in for an emergency. I called a girlfriend for a ride home and Bill headed off to the hospital.

The International House of Pancakes still has a special place in my heart because that is where Bill eventually proposed to me a few months later. Nothing fancy. No fanfare. Just a question over a plate of pancakes.

I was so excited that I forgot to answer him. Bill knew I had said yes when my mother called the next day to congratulate him and welcome him to the family.

I hadn't changed my mind about marrying him despite the fact that Bill asked me what my name was numerous times on our first trail ride—and a few times on the next ride. The trouble remembering wasn't just with MY name. It was also anniversaries, birthdays, friends' names, and more. This was a trait I would have to deal with for the rest of our relationship and through our marriage. He eventually learned my first name (though not my middle name), but people often wondered if he really was married to me, or if he was the father of our children. He couldn't remember what school, what grade, or how old our children were, but he could recite beautifully, word for word, a patient's history and lab report. That was Bill.

To celebrate our engagement and to have a change of pace from the International House of Pancakes, I asked him if I could cook him a special dinner. He talked frequently about sailing off the Northeast coast when he was in medical school, so I decided to surprise him with a lobster dinner.

I had no idea how to cook lobster. I was born and raised in Minnesota, a long way from the coast. The directions weren't in my *Betty Crocker's Picture Cook Book*, so I asked the butcher at the grocery store, where I purchased the lobsters, how to cook them. He told me to boil a big pot of water and drop the lobsters in. And when they turn red, they're done. Sounded simple to me.

Bill came to my house and he saw the big pot of boiling water on the stove.

"What are you cooking?" he asked.

"It's your surprise. Well, I guess I can tell you now. I'm cooking lobster."

"You bought live lobsters?"

"No, they're in this box. They aren't alive," I said as I went over to the kitchen counter and opened the box to show him. I didn't even get the top all the way off before I saw a claw flailing in the air. I screamed and dropped the box on the floor. The lobsters were crawling around the kitchen floor as Bill grabbed the tongs to try to catch them.

"Holy crap. They're alive!" I screamed.

"Of course they are. That's how you cook them," Bill said as he picked up one of the lobsters and placed it in my sink.

"What? They were on ice. I thought they were dead." I screamed when Bill came too close to me holding a flailing lobster in the tongs. "My family's diet is primarily vegetarian. No way. I can't drop them in boiling water. Alive!"

"They make a squealing sound when you drop them in the water," Bill said.

"Stop it. I'm going to puke," I said, as I leaned over the kitchen counter and held my head in my hands.

"Well, it really isn't a squealing sound. It is probably air being released. When they're cold, they don't move. I guess I can pith them so they won't feel the hot water. I don't know. Haven't ever done it, but I can try," he said, as I watched him chase a lobster that was heading for the kitchen table. I tried to help, but when the lobster came too close to me, I screamed.

From the dirty looks he was giving me; I could tell I was making Bill crazy. I have a loud scream. I couldn't blame him.

He crawled under the table, nabbed the last lobster, and dropped it in the sink with the others. As he was placing the tongs next to the pot of boiling water, I saw the look on his face. "You don't want to drop them in the boiling water alive either, do you?" I asked.

"No, I really don't."

I realized Bill had a big heart, whether it was for animals or people. He gathered the four lobsters and found a larger box to place them in. I felt awful about spoiling his dinner, but Bill found it funny. We took the lobsters back to the grocery store, traded them in for a bottle of wine, bread, toilet paper and other groceries we needed to offset the cost of the lobsters. Then, instead of going to my house to cook, we headed over to our favorite haunt, the International House of Pancakes.

***

Watching a sitcom on TV, I laughed as the characters had the same problem with cooking live lobsters as I had. I sympathized with them as they were chasing the critters around the room. I decided right then and there that I would go back to my *Betty Crocker's Picture Cookbook* for my next brainy idea for a surprise dinner. I'd be sure to find something you would recognize in Minnesota. But not Jell-O and hotdish, a Minnesota staple, which has cream of chicken soup, noodles, canned chicken, and peas, all topped with tater tots. Ya, for sure. You betcha!

Moses Remodels the Farmhouse

Before we got married, Bill and I bought a tar-paper shack bordered by the Zumbro River, and located on five acres at the end of a road about five miles outside of Rochester, Minnesota. There were a couple of sand pits next door that were no longer in service and filled with water. The farm had a garden, a shed, and a grain bin that was perfect for horses, chickens, and ducks.

The price was $19,000, and we purchased it from the next-door neighbor. We saw potential, which Bill's father did not. He thought we should bulldoze the house and build a new one. That wasn't in our budget. We were going to do the work ourselves, because the bones of the house seemed solid.

The first thing we purchased was a woodburning stove that we named Lord Ashley. It was our only heat source. The house was built in the early 1900s and we figured the owners added a room every time the wife was ready to deliver the next baby. It was a one and half story home with a full basement. We painted all the rooms and replaced the old linoleum flooring. We bought cedar siding and covered the tar-paper with a board and batten design. We pulled off the rickety porch with our thirty-year-old Allis-Chalmers tractor.

and replaced it with a 30- by 40-foot deck with a sunburst design, surrounded by built-in benches. In the summertime, sitting under the canopy of the hundred-year-old oak tree overhanging the deck made you temporarily forget the freezing temperatures in the winter.

The upstairs was another story. We didn't have the experience or tools to knock out walls and build dormers. We finally decided it was time to find someone willing to do the work. We contacted numerous contractors and builders, but we couldn't find anyone interested. The house was too old and unpredictable. We put an advertisement in a couple of local papers for hired help.

A few days later, a man came to the house and knocked on the door. Bill opened it and standing in front of us was a man in mismatched shoes and torn pants. His hair was down to his waist and he had a beard that went to the middle of his chest. I thought he was homeless and looking for a handout.

"I'm interested in your project," he said.

"Do you have any experience in building dormers, removing walls, and working with sheetrock?" Bill asked.

"Yep."

"Come in and I'll show you what we want to do," Bill said.

I couldn't believe Bill was taking this dude's word for it. No references. No plan. Just 'Yep.'

As the man—calling him a builder was a stretch—started upstairs to take a look, I cornered Bill.

"You're just hiring this guy when you know nothing about him?"

"Do we have a choice?"

"We're going to talk about this. Right?"

"Sure," he said as he headed up the stairs. I followed right behind him.

Bill had drawn some simple plans and showed them to the stranger. "Can you build this?" Bill asked.

"Yep."

The next thing I heard was "We'll see you tomorrow with the sledgehammer," followed by another "Yep."

The builder, whom I nicknamed "Yep," left in an old truck that took a while to start.

I was standing in the kitchen totally dumbfounded when Bill walked in.

"Did you get 'Yep's' name?" I asked. "Do you know anything about his work?"

"He's fine, and we'll get that information tomorrow."

"Oh, yes. Just great. While he's standing next to us holding a sledgehammer, you're going to grill him about his expertise and references. I feel really safe."

"I'll watch what he's doing. You don't need to worry about it."

"Hmmm. Of course, you have all the time in the world! You're only working almost a hundred hours a week in your residency. You're studying for the boards and somewhere in there, you have to eat and sleep. You're going to be leaving me with this bozo. I just know it. Even though I'm teaching full time, coaching volleyball, directing the one-act play, buying groceries, doing the laundry . . ."

Bill walked away before I finished my sentence. I slowly realized where this discussion was headed. I decided to back off and see what would happen. *Have faith* was all I could tell myself.

"It'll be fine," Bill yelled over his shoulder as he grabbed his books so he could start studying.

The next day Yep showed up in his old clunker truck with his sledgehammer, a shovel, and a wheelbarrow. He marched up the stairs and started demolishing the walls. I saw lathe and plaster flying out of the upstairs window. He was up there for hours in ninety-degree heat.

When he finally came down the stairs, I would have sworn he was a twin to the Moses character in *The Ten Commandments*. The light gray plaster dust had adhered to his long hair, beard, eyebrows, and mustache. He looked thirty years older.

"May I have a glass of water?" he asked.

"Yep," I said as I filled a glass. I couldn't help myself. I added, "Are you hungry? Do you want a sandwich?"

"Yep. Be nice."

"How's it going?" I asked, as I handed him a sandwich with some chips and an apple.

"It's good," he said. A man of few words.

He was upstairs until late in the evening pounding away at the walls. Bill came home and went upstairs to talk to him and check on his work. He had removed all the lathe and plaster in addition to two walls. A mound of boards and chunks of plaster littered the ground below the window.

"Be back tomorrow to clean up. Can I get paid for my work today?" Yep asked.

"Of course. How much do I owe you?" I asked.

"Seven dollars an hour and I worked thirteen hours," he said.

I wrote out a check for ninety-one dollars and handed it to him.

"Don't have cash?" he asked.

"No, but I can have cash available tomorrow."

"I'll get it tomorrow. Don't have a bank account."

"Okay. Will do. Thanks for your work. See ya tomorrow," I said.

He left and I decided it was okay to work with this guy. He had an excellent work ethic and was affordable.

The next day he showed up with sheetrock and everything he needed to finish the walls. The wheels on the front of his small clunker truck appeared to be slightly off the ground with the back of his truck so overloaded. He lugged each piece of heavy sheetrock up the stairs. When the truck was unloaded, he cleaned up the mound of debris on the ground and shoveled it in the back of his truck. I handed him his cash for his two days of work and asked him what he needed tomorrow. He gave me an estimate and that's how we worked. I was beginning to like this guy.

Then it was time to renovate the attic. We were removing the ceiling and putting in a cathedral ceiling with two dormer windows. Yep (I still didn't know his name) took his ladder and I followed him up the stairs to make sure he would be able to remove the ceiling without the roof caving in. I still wasn't completely sure this guy knew what he was doing.

"Do you think we can remove this ceiling?" I asked.

"Don't know. Checking it out," he said, as he set up his ladder under the small, square wooden entrance in the ceiling. He climbed the ladder, pushed aside the plank, and stuck his head into the attic. Then he pulled the rest of his body through the hole. He wasn't holding a flashlight and there was no light bulb in the attic.

"Can you see anything up there?" I asked.

"Got a lighter," he said.

Great. Let's burn the house down, I thought.

He snapped the lighter and the next thing I knew, he was coming out of the attic entrance headfirst, using his hands to descend every step of the ladder until he reached the floor.

"Can't do the job. Attic is full of spiders. Big spiders. One screamed that was too close to the lighter. They look like tarantulas."

"Spiders? Big spiders? I hate spiders," I said as a chill went through my body. "One screamed? Really?" *And I thought I had cornered the market on storytelling.*

"You have to get an exterminator. Have them vacuumed up," he said as he was going down the steps.

"Okay. Will do. Wait! When will you be back?" I asked.

"When the spiders are gone."

That night I was sitting on the couch in the living room when I noticed that the cat was batting at the curtain, which was unusual for him.

"What are you doing, Aristotle?" I asked as I headed for the curtain. He just gave me that cat look which makes you wonder what he was thinking. I pulled the curtain back and there was a spider the size of a salad plate. I screamed and got the aquarium net. I managed to catch him. He didn't try to move as I placed him in a Tupperware container on the kitchen counter. I wanted to show Bill why 'Yep' wasn't coming back and why we needed an exterminating company. He needed to believe the size of these spiders.

The next day I was able to find an exterminating company with a vacuum. Two young men arrived with a truck that had long hoses attached to a large container on the back of the truck. A gigantic vacuum. I took them upstairs and showed them the entrance to the attic.

"So, you're afraid of some little spiders," one of the guys said.

"They aren't little," I said. "I have one in a Tupperware container if you'd like to see it. My guy that's working on our project said one screamed when his cigarette lighter got too close."

"I know what a spider looks like. Screamed? That's a good one." Both guys started laughing.

"Don't you need a ladder?" I asked.

"Nope," one of the guys said as he held the legs of his partner and boosted him through the small entrance into the attic. The guy in the attic turned on his flashlight and the next thing I knew, he was coming out of the attic entrance headfirst. His buddy caught him just in time and lowered him to the floor.

"Holy sh . . .! Those spiders are huge. They look like tarantulas. I'm not going up there," he said, brushing plaster and insulation off his pants.

"Would you like a cigarette lighter to see if it screams if you get too close?" I asked, biting the inner part of my cheek so I wouldn't start laughing. "Where're you going?" I asked, as both the guys headed down the stairs.

"We're giving the boss a call to say why we can't do the job," one guy yelled back.

Soon they were back, hauling the hose up the stairs, along with a ladder. "We got to do it. Boss says."

They took the hose, placed it in the entrance, and started up the vacuum, even though they couldn't see what was being sucked up. I watched as hundreds of spiders, along with some of the old paper insulation, was sucked through the see-through hose. Every so often, one of the guys would climb up the ladder, shine a light into the attic, and suck some more. Then both men climbed into the attic to vacuum up the stragglers.

"We better check the rest of the house," one of them suggested.

"No problem. Let's check the basement first," I said. "I've only seen one in the main part of the house. I don't know where they're coming from."

They went into the far back room of the basement and headed down a small, four-foot-tall corridor that led to the well. When both of them came running out, bumping their heads on the low ceiling, I figured there were more spiders.

"Filled with spiders. The wall is about a foot thick with them. It must be where they're breeding. We need to vacuum them there, also. I think they're getting to the attic through the walls. Have your builder seal the walls."

"Do you think there are more in the house? I'm not sure I can sleep here. I'll be jumping out of bed every time I feel anything. Or I'll dream there's spiders. It'll drive my husband nuts."

"Don't know what to tell ya. I think we got them all. Not sure." These were men of few words, too.

The boys packed up the truck and left. I took the spider that was in the Tupperware container to my school and the biology teacher told me it was a Fishing Spider. They were venomous, but only if you were allergic to the bite. Fishing Spiders were unique to Minnesota and Wisconsin and liked water. No wonder they were breeding around the well.

As promised, 'Yep' came back once the spiders were gone and continued on our project. And continued, and continued. By the time he finished six months later, he had shaved his beard, cut his hair, and started wearing flashy sunglasses, khaki pants, and a polo shirt. He had a better truck and two guys working for him. He was coming up in the world.

"How much do I owe you?" I asked.

He handed me a bill with his hours and materials.

"You can write me a check. My name is Al Johnson," he said.

The job was well done and I really liked Al. He asked if he could use me as a reference and I said yes. He became a successful builder in the Rochester area and I was glad we gave him a chance. Well, I guess it was Bill that gave him the chance. I just made him lunch and paid him.

Head First and Belly Up

There is nothing like a pond in your backyard to make you feel as if you were a child again—that is, if you grew up in Minnesota, the Land of Ten Thousand Lakes. Bill and I had a pond behind our first house, on 55th St in Rochester, Minnesota. It started as a sand pit, the result of an industry that required sand. Eventually, the bulldozers left and the hole filled with water. Then, the Zumbro River overflowed and it filled with fish. Wasn't long before the birds were attracted to the fish, small game animals were attracted to the birds, and it was evolution before our eyes.

Our pond was free entertainment for a young couple with no money. That was Bill and me. In the winter, the pond became a skating rink. Well, after we shoveled two feet of snow off it. We were wary of taking machinery on the ice since we were never sure how much weight the surface could hold. The shoveling was good exercise and the pond was only an acre.

One time while we were ice skating, Bill grabbed our dog's collar and let him pull him around the ice. Charlie was a big Briard, which looks like a large sheep dog. The next thing

I knew, Bill had rigged up a rope attached to a harness that fit Charlie.

Bill brought me down to the pond to show off his invention. Charlie zipped around the ice rink and seemed to enjoy it as much as Bill. I took a spin but Charlie was a little too fast for me. I felt like I was playing Crack the Whip. Bill took his turn again and that's when the excitement hit.

Charlie was flying around the rink, Bill in tow, when a rabbit ran right in front of him. Charlie made a 90-degree turn and headed after the rabbit. Bill didn't see the rabbit and he hung on until Charlie jumped the snowbank and Bill went into the bank head first. Only his pride was hurt—that ended the pseudo dogsled experience.

When summer came, we swam., floated on rubber rafts, or took the horses for a swim. Bill built a small wooden dock with some scrap lumber we found in the barn. We would lay on the dock out in the sun with a wonderful drink by our side in total privacy. Our small farm was located on a dead-end road. It was heaven for newlyweds.

Neither Bill nor I fished, but our friend Ken loved to. One time, while Bill was at work, Ken came out to fish and brought his fresh catch of blue gills to the house to show me. I admired their iridescent color as the fish swam around in the bucket.

"What beautiful fish," I said. "I didn't know that you were catching such pretty ones."

"Do you want one?" he asked.

"Sure." I thought it would look good in Bill's sixty-liter tank with his collection of tropical fish that he'd been hauling around the country for the last five years.

Ken went back to the pond, caught another blue gill, and put it in a smaller pail for me. After he left, I took the pail over to the fish tank and dropped the blue gill inside. Swimming around, he looked a little awkward compared to the angel fish, black and cobra guppies, neon tetras and different types of sucker fish, but he seemed to fit in.

I went upstairs to fold clothes and get some work done. When I heard Bill's car coming down the driveway, I was so excited to show him the new fish. I headed down the stairs to meet him. Halfway down, I heard him yell, "What the . . .! Where are my fish?"

I ran to look in the tank. "They were just there a couple of hours ago."

"What is that? It looks like a blue gill," he said.

"Yes, it is. Ken caught him for me. I thought he'd look nice with the other fish. I named him 'Grumpy' because his lips go down in a frown. Hey, where ARE the other fish?" I asked.

"In his damn stomach. He ate them," Bill said. "I can't believe you put that fish in my tank. I've known those fish longer than I have you."

"I'm sorry. I thought he only ate worms. I didn't know he would eat your fish. I'll buy you more."

"You don't have any money and they're expensive." Bill looked at me and saw my eyes filling with tears. "I'm sorry. I didn't mean to yell at you. I'm just upset. I guess now we have an aquarium with a blue gill named Grumpy. I'll have a few words with Ken when I see him. I'm sure he thought you were going to eat him."

"Eat him? How? Just drop him in a fry pan or something? I couldn't do that."

"You've never cleaned fish?"

"No. I chopped the head off a chicken once with my mom. It ran around for a while with its head cut off. It was gross and awful. Never did that again. I feel awful about your fish. I didn't know Grumpy was a cannibal."

"You're going to have to get bait for him and feed him smaller fish or maybe hamburger."

"Are you kidding me? He doesn't eat fish flakes?"

"No, he's a wild fish. He doesn't eat fish flakes. Let's see what he does with a little hamburger."

He went over to the refrigerator and pulled out a packet of ground beef. He held a small clump of beef slightly above the water. Grumpy jumped up and ate the meat right out of Bill's fingers.

Bill jumped and so did I. "Be careful of your fingers," he said. "Maybe you should just drop small pieces in the aquarium."

"He's part piranha. I don't like him. Let's put him back in the pond."

"No, we have the most expensive blue gill on the planet and we're keeping him. You wanted him. You have him— and you'll take care of him," Bill said, giving me the look.

There was a lesson that Bill wanted me to learn: there are consequences for behaviors. Whether I'd understood the consequences beforehand didn't seem to matter to him. I couldn't believe it. I now had a fish that ate hamburger and it was my job to feed him and clean out the tank. I gag at the smell of fish. It was going to be a long, hard lesson.

But after a while, we became attached to Grumpy. He began to know us and he would come to the glass with his fin up. He appeared to be happy to see us. He would put his dorsal fin down if he was upset or had to leave his fish tank for cleaning. I would call out his name and he would come out from under his fake rock and visit. Grumpy created a lot of conversation when friends came over—a funny story at my expense. Bill forgave Ken, because he really did think I was going to eat the blue gill.

Grumpy had been with us for a couple of years, when we had the opportunity to go on a backpacking trip to the Tetons with our friends Kay and Jim Cain. I asked a number of people if they would feed him while we were gone and I couldn't get any takers. I had the great idea of going to the bait shop and buying fifty minnows. I figured he would eat a couple every day until we returned.

We were shocked when we got home. Grumpy was floating upside down and there wasn't a minnow left in the tank. He ate himself to death. I felt bad, but what a way to go. Truthfully, I was also somewhat relieved. Bill had accepted a job at the Medical University of South Carolina, Charleston, and we would be moving at the end of the summer. I had been trying to think what would happen to Grumpy. I didn't think Bill would be up for carting a blue gill halfway across the country. So, it worked out the best for everyone, maybe even Grumpy, because there was a great view of the pond from his burial site.

Lady Bird Watching

I met Kay Cain through the Mayo Clinic Fellow Wives Association, and we became great friends. Our husbands became friends, too. We backpacked in the Tetons, and canoed in the Boundary Waters.

Kay's father-in-law, Dr. Jim Cain, lived approximately a mile from our farm. Kay introduced us and we developed a warm, neighborly relationship. Dr. Cain's wife, Ida May, had the most beautiful southern accent. It was so different than my Minnesota dialect. Sometimes, to entertain my husband, I would imitate her speech and mannerisms. He would just roll his eyes and bury himself in his medical books. I couldn't help it. It was my theatrical side.

I loved it when we had the opportunity to take care of Jim and Ida May's house when they left town. The Cains had an inside, heated pool surrounded by a greenhouse. It was such a wonderful break from the cold winter and high snowdrifts of southern Minnesota. I would soak in the pool and feel so refreshed. The last time we took care of the house, I was pregnant with my first child. I didn't care that I looked like a beached whale in the pool. It was heaven.

The Cains had told me that they would be gone for a week, and this time, they would return with important guests. For security reasons, I would have to be out of the house before they arrived. As I was cleaning the house and packing my things, Dr. Cain called to tell me that they were on their way home from the airport. That's when I found out who the important people were—former President Johnson and his wife, Lady Bird. Dr. Cain was the President's personal cardiologist at the Mayo Clinic. Both families were originally from Texas and had become good friends.

I finished gathering my things as quickly as I could, threw them into my car, and headed home. Looking in the rear-view-mirror at the back seat, I saw my suitcase and realized that, in my haste, I'd left my toiletries at the house in the upstairs bathroom. I couldn't live without my makeup, hair dryer and curlers.

I turned the car around and drove back to the house. I was upstairs in the bathroom gathering my things, when I heard the front door open. I looked over the banister and saw the Cains coming through the door. There was only one set of stairs—a long, winding wooden staircase with white rails and an oriental carpet runner. The front door was across from the first step of the staircase.

"Hello, Ida May and Jim! I'm upstairs getting a few things that I left. I'll be right down and out the door," I yelled from the second floor.

"No problem. The Johnsons will be here shortly, and your timing is just right," Ida May said.

My shoes were at the front door and I was wearing nylons with my maternity dress. I started down the stairs with my belongings in my arms. I slipped on the oriental runner and slid down the steps on my back at full speed as if I were a snow toboggan.

Just when I landed at the bottom in a heap, the front door opened. My dress was above my head, and my toiletries had scattered everywhere. The Cain's visitors' welcome to the house was a set of legs in nylons covering a pregnant belly, topped by an unidentified person under a dress.

I uncovered my face to see that I was at the feet of former President Lyndon Johnson. Security was crowding around me as Dr. Cain screamed for them to get out of the way.

"Don't move," Dr. Cain told me.

"I'm sure I'm fine. I ride a horse. I'm fit. I've been falling and sliding down snow-filled hills my whole life," I said. "Just let me get up and straighten out my dress. I'm so sorry I interrupted your party."

"It's alright, darling. It was quite a greeting. Just relax and follow Dr. Cain's advice. At least one of us should," President Johnson said with a chuckle.

"Why, are you alright?" Ida May asked in her southern drawl as she leaned over my head. "I would like to introduce you to our neighbor and friend, Kathryn Gruhn. She's married to Dr. William Gruhn. Kathryn, this is President Lyndon Johnson and his wife, Lady Bird."

My perspective was very odd from my position on the floor. "Nice to meet you," I said. I didn't know what else to say.

"Ida May, get my bag." Dr. Cain said.

"Really, I'm fine." I pleaded.

Dr. Cain took his stethoscope out of his bag and listened to my stomach. He checked my arms and legs and said, "Well, there's still a strong heartbeat. I'm pretty sure you and the baby are okay, but I want you to tell your obstetrician what happened. Tell Bill, too. Will you do that for me?"

I nodded yes.

They helped me up and invited me back into the house. The Johnson's asked me about my family and farm. Then Ida May added, "And she and Bill, her husband, are taking a birding class with us."

"You're birders?" Lady Bird asked.

I couldn't honestly call myself a birder at the time. I had just bought bird feeders, suet and a couple of birding books. And I couldn't forget the phone call with Ida May just a week earlier.

"Hello, Kathryn. Will you be coming to the birding class tonight?"

"Yes, we will. Oh, you wouldn't believe what I'm looking at right now," I said as I looked out the window at one of my feeders. "It's a redheaded pecker. I haven't seen one in a while."

"Wood . . . you mean." Ida May said after a pause.

"Would I what?" I asked.

"Wood. The word has wood."

"Wood? We have some chopped wood. Do you need some?" I asked.

"No . . . the bird. The WOODpecker. You left out the word wood."

I realized what I had said and I was speechless. It was obvious I needed to brush up on my bird names. How embarrassing. And now this. Flashing the Johnsons as they arrived at the Cain's house. Sometimes, I try so hard to be prim and proper and it just isn't me.

"Do you think Bill and Kathryn would like to join us for a birding trip in Florida?" Lady Bird asked Ida May. "I have a professional birding guide. He's the best in the world. I want to complete my birding checklist during the migration period in the Everglades."

"Why, that's a wonderful idea," Ida May said. "Let's plan on it, if it's okay with Bill."

"Thank you for inviting me, and I'll certainly check with Bill," I said.

"I believe this will be an incentive for you to learn your birds," Ida May said, with a little glint in her eye and a sly smile. I'm sure she was remembering our phone call, too.

I took Ida May's advice and learned my bird names before our trip. We met the Cain's and Lady Bird in Florida and had a wonderful time. Alice, our new baby, was about two months old. It was her first birding trip. I don't know if she can count the birds on her checklist, however. She slept through most of the Everglades. As for me, I've been a true birder ever since, thanks to the Cains and Lady Bird.

Moving to the Carolinas

Floating Cars and Porcupines

If there was one thing Bill and I loved to do in our younger years, it was hiking—whether we camped or backpacked. We could each carry over fifty pounds on our backs as we trudged around mountains, hills, or waterways. We didn't have money, but we had stamina. I loved the views from the mountaintops that weren't available to me growing up as a flatlander in Minnesota. Bill grew up in southern California and had the Sierra Nevada range at his disposal.

Shortly before our big move south to Charleston, South Carolina, we planned a camping trip to the Bighorns in northeast Wyoming. Bill had hiked there when he took a trip to the Black Hills, in southwest South Dakota. The two parks aren't far apart. We loaded Bill's Datsun B210 hatchback with our tent, sleeping bags, hatchets, camp stove, food, water, and clothes. I made sure Bill had extra pants and shoes, since we'd had a problem with that in the past.

We stopped and visited Bill's parents on their farm in Huron, South Dakota, since it was the half-way point to our destination, and they had agreed to take care of our daughter, Alice, who was six months old at the time. We would be gone for a long weekend.

We took off early for the Bighorns the following morning with our coffee in hand and had fun reading the Wall Drug billboards lining the highway. Wall Drug is a welcoming tourist trap in the middle of South Dakota. We stopped long enough to see the taxidermy bucking bronc that had been there for 50 years. Bill and his sister had had their picture taken on it when they were kids.

Most of the souvenirs are made in China. I've always wondered what the Chinese thought while they were making Indian and cowboy figurines. For many years, when I taught English as a Second Language, Asian men would ask me where they could see cowboys and Indians. I would say, "Go west, young man, go west, and stop at Wall Drug."

During our trip, Bill and I stopped at a number of small roadsides stands to buy rocks, fossils, and arrow heads. Each place had rattlesnake hides hanging from the makeshift roofs. Some were as long as eight feet. I swear the westerners got a kick out of watching flatlanders, who grew up with no poisonous snakes, squirm.

Maybe I saw too many National Geographic documentaries when I grew up, because I was more nervous than most. I still had visions of all that rattle-shaking, body-coiling and, of course, striking. Bill and I saw a lot of rattlesnakes as we hiked, and I jumped every time. Once I moved to the Carolinas, I had to live with copperheads, but they don't coil and strike. They just lay there waiting for you to step on them or accidently grab them while weeding the garden. I've picked up many with the pitchfork and thrown them out of the way. No big deal.

We approached the Bighorns National Forest on the east side by way of highway US 14. A vertical relief of over 8000 feet, straight up from the plains, greeted us. The Bighorns are above the tree line, with a coniferous forest below. In the higher areas (Cloud Peak, at 13,175 feet), snowstorms can occur well into June and July. Of course, I didn't know it then.

The park, at 200,000 acres, was huge. The trails were remote, and most of them had limited rangers and buildings, so it was important to pack correctly. I didn't know that either.

We entered the park through a small, open metal gate. It was the beginning of June and clearly the season wasn't in full swing. Bill traversed the bumpy dirt road and at times I didn't know if his Datsun would make it. A four-wheel drive vehicle would've been the smart way to go, I thought. Too late now. We came to a creek, and I was afraid we would have to turn around.

"This car floats, and anyway, that creek isn't that deep. I'm driving across it. I have a favorite campsite that's further up the mountain," Bill said.

"I sank my uncle's truck in a creek like that. I think we better turn around. There's no way we'd get a wrecker in here to retrieve it." My internal warning lights were blinking.

"I know what I'm doing," he said. *Uh-huh, I've heard that before.*

Bill backed up the car, revved the motor, and hit the accelerator hard. The little Datsun skidded across the water to the other side and kept chugging up the slippery dirt road.

"Told ya" was all he said. I could see he was enjoying the win.

We stopped at his campsite spot on the top of a ridge where the tree line was getting sparse. The view was incredible. Bill and I unpacked the car and set up camp.

I started supper with a campfire glowing next to me. Bill took his fishing rod and was off to catch dinner. "I'll be down by Goose Creek if you need me," he said.

"Okay." I was humming Girl Scout songs as I put freeze-dried packets of macaroni and cheese in a pot on our Coleman stove and added water. The campfire was perfect for Bill's catch of the day.

When I heard some commotion behind me and turned around, I was face-to-face with a huge, bristly-looking grizzly bear cub. I jumped, screamed, and ran towards the river, shrieking every time I tripped and fell in rutted moose tracks.

"Bill, Bill, we have a grizzly bear cub in our camp. Help!" I yelled as soon as I spied him by the river.

"There aren't grizzlies here," he shouted back.

"The hell! There's one in our camp and it's after our food. Or maybe it thinks I'm food. I'm not going back without you."

"I haven't caught any fish yet."

"Screw the fish. What if it attacks the car? We may never get out of here."

Bill packed up his fishing gear and headed to the campsite. I hid behind him, hoping he would be the first one for bear bait. When we arrived at the camp, the animal was waddling around, minding his own business as he helped himself to our macaroni and cheese.

"It's a giant porcupine," Bill said. "Not a grizzly cub. Wow, you made me come back for that?"

"Well, if you think it's so harmless, why don't you just mosey over there and nicely talk it into leaving the camp and our dinner," I said, trying not to sound too sarcastic. "Please?"

Bill picked his fishing pole back up and headed toward the beast. "Come along now. Time to leave," he said in his sweetest voice.

When the porcupine noticed Bill, he blew up about twice his size. I swear those quills were a foot long. The porcupine stood his ground and Bill stood his.

Then, the porcupine headed for Bill. He started backing up as fast as he could—until he hit a rut and fell. I ran to the back of the car and grabbed the car jack, the spare tire, and a shovel. I threw them at the porcupine, screaming the whole time. He took one look at me, turned around, and left the camp.

"I think you've scared off every living creature in the whole park," Bill said.

"The next time I'll take a picture with you covered in porcupine quills." I guess I thought I deserved a thank you or something. I was peeved.

"Let's hike up to the top of this mountain for the sunset," he said, as he wiped the mud off his pants. "We can take some Gorp and eat dinner afterwards."

"I'm in on that," I said. as I cleaned up the half-eaten food while Bill rescued his car jack and spare tire.

We hiked a little higher up to an overlook that was amazing. We ate some Gorp, took a swig of water, and just enjoyed the sunset. It was breathtaking. The shadows changed the color of the foliage to bright reds, oranges, and golds. It was so peaceful. This was the reason we came on the trip, I thought.

We went back to the campsite, cooked more mac and cheese, and snuggled in our warm tent after we ate. We'd had enough excitement for one day.

The next morning, Bill headed out with his fishing pole and camera. I stayed back at the campsite to cook and read. The weather was chilly and the wind was picking up. I sensed that maybe a storm was brewing.

Later that afternoon, when Bill made it back to the campsite, he had a story to tell me.

"I was walking along a small path next to a shallow lake when I heard some splashing. I looked across the lake and saw a large bull moose with an enormous set of antlers." He outstretched his arms and his eyes were wide. "The moose was drinking at the edge of the lake, and I snuck down and started taking pictures. That huge moose crossed the lake and went after me. He chased me up the path and I had to climb a tree. The moose rammed the trunk for quite a while before he got tired and walked away. I thought I was going to die." Bill said. I had my doubts about the size of the moose and the fact that Bill actually climbed a tree, but it was a good story.

We ate and went to bed after laughing about the moose and the porcupine. When we woke up, there was six inches of snow on the ground.

"Bill, there's snow!" I shouted when I peeked out of the tent.

"That's what I love about this park. Don't worry, it'll warm up, and we'll be able to hike some. That's how it is. Freezing cold at night and warm during the day."

Sure enough, the snow started melting, and we were able to get in a small hike. By the next morning—our last day at the park—the snow was gone. We packed up the car and headed back the way we came. The creek, the Datsun had valiantly crossed, was now a raging river.

"Wow, what happened to the creek?" I asked.

"Snow melt. Don't worry. This car floats," Bill insisted.

He gunned the car. It made it two-thirds of the way across, before it started sinking. The strong current caused the car to drift towards the large lake the creek emptied into. I was ready to jump out and head for shore.

"Here, grab the steering wheel and get in my seat while I get rocks under tires," Bill shouted as he jumped out the driver's door.

"Are you crazy? We're going to drown and they'll never find us sunk in that lake. No way!" I realized I was the only one left in the car and the lake was fast approaching. I did as I was told.

Bill was throwing rocks under the tires as I kept slamming down the gas pedal. "We're not going to make it." I screamed, opening the driver's door.

"Gun it! Stay in the car!" Bill slammed the door shut and grabbed another rock.

I gunned it again and we were closer to the other side. Little by little we made it, but the side of the creek was slippery and the car was having difficulty getting up the riverbank. Bill went behind and pushed the car up the bank. Don't ask me how he got the strength. I was the one that always opened the pickle jars.

"I told you the car floated. It was just that the water was rushing too fast," he said.

"Ya, sure. Tell that to the Datsun dealer and I'm sure he would put you in a commercial."

We kept that car a long time, even though the passenger door was tied with baling twine, the bumpers were secured with duct tape, and the windshield had four cracks that made the driver have to crick his neck in order to see. The bottom of the car was completely rusted from the Minnesota winters.

Bill told him he couldn't park the car in the doctor's parking lot. His superiors said his car was embarrassing. So, Bill traded the car for a Peugeot. I named it 'Peez-uv-zhit', which I pronounced in my best French accent. I hated that car. It was in the shop more often than in our garage, and not dependable like the Datsun, but Bill loved it. That's all that mattered.

***

A couple of months later, I processed the photos from our trip out west. The pictures from Bill's photo shoot with the bull moose were amazing. The camera must have been in automatic mode. The first couple of pictures, you see the moose drinking; in the next sequence, the moose is lifting his head in Bill's direction; in the third group, the moose is crossing the lake towards Bill. Then I started laughing out loud, because the next picture was taken at a cock-eyed angle that shows the moose splashing through the water in close proximity. And the final sequence is a picture of Bill's feet, followed by one of the trail, and, finally, the tree limb he had to climb.

And all that time he was telling me the story during our trip, I thought he was exaggerating. Now he has the pictures to prove it.

Minnesota Out, Carolina In

Bill and I arrived in the beautiful city of Charleston, South Carolina, in the fall of 1979. The town was a far cry from Rochester, Minnesota, but I was up for an adventure. Our daughter, Alice, was eight months old, and I was playing the mother role diligently. She was allergic to dairy, so I continued to nurse her. Nursing this long wasn't always an accepted practice at that time, so I was referred to as a hippie mom. Research on the advantages of mother's milk wasn't yet available. For me, nursing was far easier than washing and preparing bottles in the middle of the night.

Driving down Highway 61 from Charleston to Middleton Place Plantation, where I boarded my horse, was magical. The Spanish moss hung low on the oak trees that were hundreds of years old and overhung the highway. The temperature was in the upper 70's, which was heavenly compared to Minnesota in November. The air was filled with the scent of the ocean breeze, but if the wind was blowing in the wrong direction, you would get a whiff of the paper mill. The azaleas, wax myrtles, oleander, and tea olives provided color and fragrance that was sweet and delicious. Against the sage colors of the trees and grasses, the perennial flowers jumped out as if they were on center stage. The swamp grass was so different from the alfalfa fields in Minnesota.

The two things South Carolina did have in common with Minnesota? It was flat and there were plenty of mosquitos. I soon learned the biggest difference between the two states— Minnesota didn't have any wild creatures that slithered on the ground that could kill you.

I think that might be why the Minnesotans stay and tolerate the cold and snow. I get it. Up North there are no alligators, cotton mouths, copperheads, rattlers, Eastern diamond backs, black widows, and brown recluse spiders. But more importantly, no obnoxious palmetto bugs! I still think the name doesn't fit those big, black cockroaches that can fly. The name is too dignified for those fast little boogers. I was thrilled when I found a cat at the Humane Society that would kill them. It was wonderful. I couldn't spray any insecticide, because I had a baby crawling on the floor.

In South Carolina, I also had to keep the toilet seats closed at all times. Why?

Sewer rats. I had a family of sewer rats that had babies in the attic above my dining room. They didn't make any sound when the exterminators first arrived, so I offered the boys lunch. As the two men were eating, they heard the pitter-patter above their heads and the squeaking from the babies. "You've got rats alright. Big rats!" One of the men said with wide open eyes and his mouth pinched shut.

They walked into the bathroom. The other guy said, "Keep the lid closed on the toilet, ma'am. That's how these critters get in your house. We'll be back to treat the area from the outside." I tried to follow their instructions. Oh, how I tried. But it was a challenge, being married to a man who left the toilet seat up in the middle of the night. Nightmares, anyone?

To take our minds off all these vermin, Bill and I would take Alice and walk along the Battery, which is located at the end of the peninsula in the city of Charleston. It was a lovely place, lined with homes from the eighteenth century. The history was amazing. Charleston was founded in 1670 as Charles Town, honoring King Charles II of England. Ten years later it became Charleston, the fifth largest city in the United States. We lived in a house on Trad Street, close to where it intersected with King Street. The house was easy to find. I just had to look for a home that leaned to the right, like the leaning tower of Pisa. Yep, that was our rental house. Our yard backed up to First Scots Presbyterian Church's graveyard, which often was Alice's playground. I was desperate for her to get some fresh air and there were no playgrounds close by. She turned out okay and she isn't afraid of ghosts or grave robbers.

Heading down to the Battery from our house, I would look out over the sea wall and imagine the battles, or the pirates that were hung there. Now, yachts and sailboats enter the harbor peacefully. I would tour the houses, gardens and small walkways while pushing Alice in her wooden stroller that I had bought at an antique shop. Sitting in the courtyard outside of the café at the Mills House, I had my first she-crab soup. It's made from the female crab and cooked in cream and sherry. The almond and chocolate croissants with espresso replaced the doughnuts and black coffee from the local bakery in Minnesota. I didn't think anything could rival the Blooming Prairie Bakery, where overalls and barn boots were most welcomed. Walking down the street, I felt as though I should be wearing a hoop skirt, corset, and buttoned-up shoes.

My entertainment was riding in the Middleton Place Hunt. We became members and I developed lifelong friends. I shipped my husband's Appaloosa down from Minnesota—the same horse that Bill rode when I first met him. We had to keep Sian because he was so wild, no one would buy him. Bill and I shared him and we each were able to ride one day a week to the Middleton Hounds.

Every Tuesday and Saturday during the fall and winter months, Middleton Place Plantation held a fox hunt called a drag. No, people didn't dress in drag! It's a style of foxhunting. A person who is familiar with the hunt country—either the huntsman or a staff member—goes out about an hour before the hunt and lays down fox scent. He dunks a sandbag, which is attached to a rope, into a bucket of fox scent and drags it behind a horse while going down the trail at a walk or slow trot. Would you believe there is a company in Pennsylvania that sells this stuff? When it's shipped, the post office keeps it behind the building because it REALLY stinks—a strong, musky smell. One time the huntsman told me he had overslept and was in a hurry. He took off at a gallop. The sandbag flew in the air and hit the horse in the rear end. The horse took off bucking. The huntsman hit the ground and had to chase his horse back to the stable. What's the saying? Oh, yeah, "Haste makes waste."

The only time I had trouble in the foxhunt was the time the sound of one of the hounds replicated the cry of my baby, Alice. My milk let down and two wet spots began to grow on the front of my hunting jacket. As we were standing at a check point listening to the hounds' work, I told one of the girls who was riding with me what was happening. She jokingly told me that the hounds would smell it and attack me. Not knowing she was kidding, I panicked and told the Field Master, Mrs. Rivers, that I needed to leave, but didn't know my way around the hunt country.

"Can anyone take Mrs. Gruhn back to the stables?" the Field Master asked.

"I'll show her the way home," a voice from a man in the field piped up.

It was Ross Hanahan, who happened to own Millbrook Plantation, which was located next to Middleton Plantation. He was riding a seventeen-hand, solid black Friesian with a flowing mane and feathers on his fetlocks. The horse's nostrils were flared and he had a wild look in his eyes, matching the wild look in Ross's eyes that went perfectly with his wild hair that flowed out from under his helmet.

"He's a little crazy. Look out," a woman riding next to me said under her breath.

I'd met Ross only once at a hunt breakfast, so I had no way of knowing that he had no fear—and no sense. He started off at a dead run down the road and I quickly followed him. I caught up and noticed that he looked like

Gene Wilder on horseback, wide-eyed with a big grin. He gave his horse a kick and pulled ahead of me.

The hunt country covered almost ten thousand acres and most of the trails consisted of old logging roads. All of a sudden, a wild boar came flying out of the woods between me and Ross. My horse slammed on the brakes and we were face to face with a wild, black, pig with spikey hair and tusks. He was about three feet tall with a skinny rear end and he was looking at me and my horse straight on. It was the first time I had seen a wild boar and I was scared to death.

"Ross!" I screamed at the top of my lungs. I have a tremendous scream.

Ross turned around, saw the wild boar and headed right for him at a dead run. The boar heard the pounding hoofbeats and turned to see what was behind him. Ross played a game of chicken with him and Ross won. The wild boar took off into the brush. I guess it sensed that Ross was fearless.

By this time the front of my jacket was completely soaked. Ross stopped and looked at me. "Did you know that your coat is wet? Did one of your fake boobs blow open?"

"No, Ross, I don't have fake boobs. I'm a nursing mother," I said.

"What does nursing your mother have to do with your wet coat?"

"Ross, just get me home, fast,"

"I know a shortcut. Follow me," he said.

This should have been my first clue that there was going to be trouble. We went a few feet off the trail onto another path that wasn't very wide. I suspect it was a deer trail. The small path twisted and turned and at times it was hard to find. After about a half hour, Ross stopped. "We're lost. I thought this was going to go to another road. We better head back and find the road."

By now, my coat was completely drenched and I was uncomfortable with his idea. But what could I do? I was dependent on Ross to get me back to the stable. I continued to follow him and we came to a huge ravine. We could see the road on the other side. I came up to the edge, only to see the creek below was filled with alligators. "Ross, we can't cross this creek. It's filled with alligators."

"No problem." The next thing I knew, Ross turned his horse around and walked back about fifty feet. I began to follow him, assuming he was finding another route. He turned, kicked his horse, and came at that gorge at a dead run. He jumped it, but his horse's hind feet didn't quite make it and the horse had to scramble up the bank to safety. I was holding my breath and visualizing a horrible ending. I watched as the horse clawed his way to the top. Ross turned him around.

"Okay, your turn. It's doable," he yelled from the other side.

Sian was dancing, his front feet alternating in the air. He didn't want to be left behind. I was screaming, "No way. I'm not...."

I turned my horse around to find another way. But Sian had other ideas. He made a 180-degree turn and headed for that gorge. I couldn't stop him. I closed my eyes and hung on. Unlike Ross's horse, he cleared the ravine with no problem.

I opened my eyes once while I was in midair. The memory of those alligators below me remains with me to this day. Sian, the Appaloosa (sometimes referred to as the App-to-lose-it) was a naughty horse at times, but at that moment, I thought he was a saint.

"I'm glad your horse can jump," is all Ross said as he headed down the road.

For once I was speechless. Being gator lunch wasn't on my bucket list. I was glad to be alive.

Guarding Richard Simmons

When I was in my early thirties, I volunteered for a committee to raise funds for the Muscular Dystrophy Association (MDA) to be held at the old Convention Center in Charlotte, North Carolina. My responsibilities included bringing Richard Simmons, a TV talk-show host, who was a weight and exercise mystic, to the community. With his short stature, Afro hair, and feminine mannerisms, he was unique and very different from the other, much more macho, male exercise coaches. Women seemed to love him. Because I exercised regularly and was comfortable wearing a leotard, the other physicians' wives voted for me to be on stage with Richard during his performance and to be his chaperone when he entered and exited the stage at the Convention Center. This sounded like fun and an easy job for me.

I had seen Richard Simmons on television many times and never understood what women saw in him. He was always jumping around, laughing with the audience, and creating new food ideas. To better understand him, I went to the bookstore and bought his cookbook. Sharing his recipes with your gourmet group wouldn't be the best idea—they didn't have any sugar, salt, fat, or other good stuff in them.

The entrée pictures looked pretty, but I went straight to the desserts. The ones I tried weren't edible. I learned from the cookbook's foreword that Richard had been overweight in childhood, and as a result, was bullied, which was why he encouraged people to get fit and lose weight, a philosophy that helped many women and perhaps a few men as well. I had more respect for him after I knew his story.

The day arrived for the scheduled event at the convention center. It was a full afternoon of books, T-shirts, mugs, and poster sales. Richard Simmons paraphernalia was everywhere. The venues were packed with women buying Richard's latest cookbook, which I'm sure they were all hoping to get signed. Most of the women I saw at the event were overweight, which I like to refer to as fluffy, but the girls were full of enthusiasm. The idea was to have Richard on a raised stage on the main floor with two women, his assistant, and I, following his routines. The floor in front of him contained hundreds of women exercising and being entertained. From my spot, all I could see was Richard's backside and thousands of arms and legs in the audience swinging every which way.

I was surprised to see a different side of Richard. He pointed to a beautiful woman in the front row who had hair down to her knees. He said, "You should spend more time on exercising and less time on your hair." The woman left. I could tell by her expression she wasn't happy. He kept turning around and snapping at us with comments such as, "Do something. I'm sick of this sh…!" "Do you know how long I've been on the road?" "God help me!"

I'm sure staying in hotels, traveling, and performing the same routine over and over would get old, I thought, but his paycheck was pretty hefty.

All of a sudden, while he was doing a dance, he announced, "I want some men up here to exercise!" His assistant and I had to find volunteers in the audience, which wasn't easy because the place was mostly filled with women. We managed to find four men who agreed to come on stage.

Richard started exercising, yelling out the next move as he went, and the men tried to follow. The routine lightened up the show and the guys were goodhearted enough to laugh with the crowd. Then Richard turned around and jumped on one of the male volunteers, wrapping his arms around the guy's neck and his legs around his waist. The guy, a big, muscular, southern redneck, stopped exercising.

I could see there was going to be a confrontation. I ran up to Richard and yelled, "I'll catch you before you fall." When Richard jumped off, he saw the guy's angry face. I whispered in the guy's ear that this was a gag to get the audience laughing. I thanked him for being a great sport. I could tell by his furrowed expression that he had his doubts.

I made it look as if this had been a staged act, and the performance continued smoothly. The women were enjoying themselves—Richard was easy to follow and a little more jovial since he'd avoided being beaten to a pulp. Looking at his watch, Richard turned to me and asked, "Where's my police escort to get me out of here?"

"I'm your escort," I said, trying to talk and exercise at the same time.

"You? Are you kidding me? Get a policeman!"

"We weren't told to have a policeman available for you. The security guards are managing the crowd, and I don't think they're personally responsible for you. I can ask, however," I said. Here I was doing my best to keep up with the routine, trying to talk while I was leaping up and down and moving from side to side. Police escort? I thought he was overreacting.

"Those slobs are going to control the crowd? Too late for help now. I'm doing this last dance as an encore and then I'm outta here. Where's the elevator?" Richard asked, looking around.

"It's that way. The same one we came down when we left the green room," I said, pointing in the general direction. "I'm sure we'll be fine."

Richard gave me a dirty look, and I didn't say anything else.

The last song played and he raised his hands in the air and told the girls in the audience to do the same thing. "Take a big breath and blow it out. Slowly."

I turned to his assistant and whispered, "Did he say, 'take a big breast'?"

She laughed and then we both got the giggles. Richard started waving goodbye, blowing kisses, and screaming how much he enjoyed it. He left the stage and headed for the elevator. We were walking quickly behind him, laughing, when all of a sudden Richard yelled, "Run! They're coming!" I looked behind me and saw what must have been at least a hundred women rushing towards us. They were big and sturdy and could easily have knocked us over.

I ran past Richard, reached the elevator first, and pressed the button. The sound of the women was deafening as they screamed his name and rushed past the security guards. Richard and his assistant scooted behind me as I stretched my arms and legs out in a jumping jack position inside the elevator, blocking the entrance, all one hundred and ten pounds of me protecting them. I shouted to the women crowding toward me as I frantically pressed the 'close door' button, "Stop! Now! Or you will be prosecuted. This is private property!"

The women stopped just long enough for the elevator door to almost close. One woman stuck her hand in between the closing doors to try to pry the door open. I slapped her hand away. Richard and his assistant were huddled behind me. Fortunately, the door shut.

I can't print the words that Richard was using. Now, I fully understood why he wanted a police escort. The assistant and I kept quiet while he vented. We reached the top floor and I took him to the green room stocked with food and beverages. He calmed down and turned to me.

"What did you mean by saying 'this is private property'?"

"Well, I didn't think it would be proper to say, 'We'll shoot if you come any closer'."

He laughed and all ended well. We were able to donate a nice chunk of change to the Muscular Dystrophy Association and I counted my blessings. Richard was safe. His assistant was fun, and I had the opportunity of playing a police officer. However, a couple of hours was enough for me.

Say What?

Shortly after Bill and I moved to Charlotte, North Carolina, I found a job as a speech pathologist working for a home health agency. I saw patients ranging from newborn babies to adults in their golden years and everything in-between. Helping my professional colleagues from surrounding universities, I took in interns to give them experience. Since I had such a wide range of patients and disabilities, it was easy for an intern to gain all the required hours to receive certification from the American Speech and Hearing Association. This was giving back, since someone had done that for me.

One of these interns, Annette, who was as sweet and charming as can be, lived locally, and was enrolled in the master's program at Appalachian State University. She was thrilled that I was willing to take her on as an intern for the spring semester. The first month, she followed me and took notes while I taught her the whats, whens and whys of speech, language, stuttering, and swallowing—along with all the anatomy and physiology that went along with each disorder. One of my referrals was an African-American woman who had had a stroke and needed an evaluation.

Annette was with me to observe the full evaluation and I told her I would answer any questions that came up.

"Okay, Annette," I said. "Here's the order of an evaluation: medical history, articulation test, Minnesota Aphasia Inventory, oral-motor examination and swallowing ability. I just want you to watch what I do until I feel you're able to conduct the evaluation yourself. Are you on board?"

"Yes, that'll be great," she said.

When we arrived at the woman's house, her daughter let us in. "I have to run an errand," she said. "Is it okay if I leave you with my mother and go?"

"Is your mother verbal enough to be able to answer some simple questions?" I asked.

"Oh, yes. I think it'll be no problem. She's opinionated, but she knows why you're here."

"I have no problem with that. Most adults are opinionated," I said with a chuckle.

Her mother was sitting in a recliner in the living room. The room was decorated with multiple vases of plastic flowers and pictures of Jesus. The smell of ancient tobacco smoke radiated from the walls, from which the paint was peeling.

I went over and sat next to her on the couch. Annette joined me. "Hello, Mrs. Washington. I've been sent here to help you recover from a stroke."

"Give me a damn cigarette and I'll recover a lot faster," she said. "Shit, get old and they treat you like a baby. Sick of this! I'm tired of people telling me what to do. I just want to be left alone with some peace and quiet."

I could tell this evaluation was going to take a while and I would have to finesse to get the information I needed. At least, I could tell her language skills didn't need any work. I looked at Annette and knew she was relieved I was the one evaluating this woman.

"I agree with you, Mrs. Washington. That's why I am going to make this visit short and sweet. It's required by Medicare for me to evaluate you and make sure you're okay. You had some problems in the hospital after the stroke. You were referred to home health for me to follow up on your progress."

"Okay, go on with it." I could tell from the disgusted look on her face how she felt about our visit.

"Mrs. Washington, I see you weren't on any medication before you went to the hospital. Can you tell me what happened or how you felt prior to your stroke?" I asked.

"I was vomiken and fallen' off."

"Vomiken" and falling off? I looked around, wondering what she had been falling off of. Did she hit her head and actually have a head injury and not a stroke?

I turned to Annette. "I'm going to pursue this a little further, I want to make sure her diagnosis is correct."

"Exactly what did you fall off of, Mrs. Washington?" I asked. "And what is vomiken? I'm not so sure I know what that means."

"I ain't fallen off a nothin'," she said with a puzzled look on her face. "I can walk and sit with no problem. You don't know what vomiken is? How can you be in medicine and not know that?"

Annette leaned over and whispered, "Vomiken is vomiting and 'fallen' off' is a local term that the older African-American community uses. It means losing weight." Annette grew up in the area and was familiar with the colloquial language.

"Gotcha, okay," I whispered back. I turned to Mrs. Washington. "So, you were vomiting and losing weight." I said, noting this on my paper to put in her report. "Let's get to the next question.

"What did you do for a living, Mrs. Washington?" I wanted to get an idea of her past jobs and ability so I didn't overtax her with formal testing. I could tell she was already tired of talking to me.

"I draw," she said.

I looked around and didn't see any paintings, charcoal drawings or artistic evidence whatsoever. I was confused, so I decided to get more specific.

"Did you use pencil?" I asked.

"No."

"Paints?" I mimicked painting with a brush.

"No. Not done that."

"Charcoal drawings?"

"Say what? Don't know what that is," she said, glaring at me with her good eye on the right side of her face.

"Colored pencils?"

She shook her head 'no'.

"Chalk? Ink?" She kept shaking her head 'no'. I was trying to think of anything she could possibly use to draw a picture or a portrait.

"Exactly what do you draw?" I asked.

"I'm not telling you what the government pays me! What kind of kook are you? Don't know medicine and now you're asking me how much money I make?" She took a bite of her sandwich and a sip of her water before blasting out, "I'm done with you! I ain't telling you what I draw!"

I turned and looked at Annette. I could tell she was busting a gut trying to hold back her laughter.

My reputation was shot, and obviously Mrs. Washington didn't have any problem communicating or swallowing. This evaluation was over.

Raising Children in Charlotte

Funniest Person in America

Fundraising for the Muscular Dystrophy Association (MDA) doesn't sound like an activity that would lead to another story, but trust me, it did. I was on the board of the Mecklenburg Medical Wives at the time, and we were given the opportunity to be a part of the 1983 Funniest Person in America contest sponsored by Show Time. We contacted many professional comedians and ended up with twenty-six contestants, all men. The winner would be given a five-minute video spot in between scheduled movies on a cable television network. This was a big deal. And our local branch of the MDA would get a portion of the funds collected from the contest ticket sales. It was a win-win situation.

The day arrived for the event and my co-sponsor, Nancy, and I were sitting at the sign-up table, busily registering the comedians. The agenda and rules were given, with emphasis on the fact that, when the light flashed, each comedian had twenty seconds to wrap up his five-minute comedy routine.

We were almost finished with the final contestant's registration when Nancy asked me a question. "Was this contest only open to male comedians?"

"No, we just didn't have any women apply."

"Well, you know," the final contestant interrupted, "women aren't funny. They're only good comediennes if they're fat, ugly, or potty-mouthed. I figured you girls would know that. Anyway, men don't want to hear a bunch of whiny bitches." He looked at the both of us, a sly grin on his face.

"Really? Well, I'll have you know that my friend here, Kathy, is funnier than hell and she isn't fat, ugly, or potty-mouthed. So, you're wrong about that," Nancy said, pointing to me.

"Sure. Ya. You sure look like you could be funny," he said sarcastically. "Maybe you could jump up and down a few times on a pogo stick and have those pearls hit you in the face. You may get a laugh out of that." He walked away laughing.

"And he's funny? You have to show him. I'll contribute a $100 to our fundraiser if you get up there for five minutes. Tell some of your jokes and stories. I'd like to show that smart-ass that pretty women are funny," Nancy said. "That guy really pisses me off."

"No way! I'm not doing that. I'm a doctor's wife, not a comedienne. And I'm a speech pathologist who teaches for a living. Forget it. As far as I'm concerned, he's right."

"You're just chicken-shit," Nancy said. "I can't believe you'd let a guy talk about women like that and not stand up for your rights. You aren't acting like the Kathy I know."

"I can't believe you said that. You do it! I'm busy running the show. Or just ignore him," I said.

"No, you need to prove him wrong. What happened to the Kathy that sang, 'I am Woman, Hear Me Roar'? Tell some Ole and Lena jokes. Some of your funny true stories. Come on. You can do it. I'm willing to put my money where my mouth is." Nancy egged me on with her every word. "At least represent your fellow sisters. Maybe you would inspire some girl to become a comedienne. Think about it!"

"No! Well . . . maybe. Okay. Sign me up. I'll tell the producer our plan."

I found the producer and told him I wanted to compete.

"You have to sign some permission forms to be videotaped and to agree to give the cable company the rights to your comedy routine," he said.

"No problem. I'm not going to win anyway. I'm just doing this on a bet."

Nancy came running up to me. "They drew names and you're the first one. You only have twenty minutes before you go on stage."

"Oh, my. Doesn't look like I have time to finish the paperwork," I said to the producer.

"Go ahead and get ready and we'll have you sign the papers when you're done. That is, if you win," the producer said with a grin.

I started laughing. "Fat chance!"

"The comedians are in Ballroom A. Hurry!" Nancy said.

When I walked into Ballroom A, the male comedians were all pacing back and forth and talking to themselves.

"Hey, has anyone heard Leena and Ole jokes? I have a really funny one," I said.

"Shut the hell up! We're practicing our scripts," a guy yelled back.

I ran back to the registration desk. "Nancy, I have to have a script! I'm going out to the car to get a pad and pencil."

"You don't need a script. Just be yourself," she yelled, but I didn't listen.

I ran to my old 1979 Suburban and rummaged around, looking for a pad of paper. I had teaching materials, tools, toys, clothes, toiletries, old food bags and a garbage bag, but no paper. I stuffed the garbage bag with loose items, hoping to find paper underneath the junk. Then I had an epiphany. I'd bring the garbage bag on stage and tell a joke or story about whatever I pulled out of the bag. Brilliant! I ran back to Ballroom A carrying my garbage bag. The men were concentrating so hard that no one noticed.

"Kathryn Gruhn, you're on stage. Follow me. How should I introduce you?" the producer asked as we approached the stage.

"Just say my name and that I'm a . . . wife . . . mom . . . teacher?"

"Okay. That's different, but whatever." He grabbed the microphone. "Here's our first contestant, Kathryn Gruhn. She is a wife, mother, and teacher. Give her a hand."

The audience clapped and then he handed me the microphone, which I immediately dropped.

"Sorry, I didn't know it was so heavy," I said. The audience laughed. I think they thought it was part of my routine. "Hi. I'm winging this. So, whatever I pull out of this black bag, I'm going to tell a joke or story about it. Here I go!"

I reached in the bag and pulled out an English book. "I was introduced as a teacher. I work with people that want to change their dialect and speak conversational English. Let me tell you what happened when I was working with a family from Japan. When I knocked on the door at the address my boss gave me, I was met by a woman and her husband. She bowed and handed me a pair of men's slippers that must have been a size twelve. They don't wear shoes in the house in Japan, so I followed their custom out of respect. As I unzipped my right boot, my nylon shredded to pieces, leaving my foot fully exposed. The woman of the house stared and bowed again. I got my other foot out of my boot with no problem and placed my feet into the slippers. As soon as I started walking, my left foot slid right out of the slipper. I reinserted my foot and shuffled to the dining room table with my English books in my arms. I had to concentrate so I didn't step out of the slippers." I shuffled across the stage, imitating my funny walk and bowing. "The man and woman were bowing on each side of me. I felt like royalty, and then the Japanese lady said, 'Betty Wodge.'

"'No,' I told her, "My name is Kathy Gruhn."

'Betty Wodge,' the woman said again, a little more slowly.

"I don't know Betty. I'm your teacher. My name is Kathy Gruhn. Say it after me, K-a-t-h-y G-r-u-h-n." I said, face to face and emphasizing every letter in my name.

The woman looked at me and pointed to the slippers. 'Betty wodge.'

"'Oh!' I said, biting my lip so I wouldn't laugh. "Yes. Very large! Yes. The slippers are very large."

The audience burst into laughter. This put me right at ease. "Ready for another one?" I asked. My question was met with whistles, clapping, and cheering.

I stuck my hand in the bag and pulled out a Tampax box. I quickly stuffed it back in the bag, but the people in the front row saw it.

"You can't do that. You said you'd tell a story about anything you pulled out of the bag. No cheating!" a guy yelled. His girlfriend nodded in agreement as the audience started chanting. "Cheater, cheater."

"Okay. Okay. Calm down. I'll tell a story. This happened to me just the other day.

"I went into a CVS to buy some things and ended up in line behind a young girl at the counter who was buying a box of Tampax. She looked around twelve years old and I thought this might be the first time she ever bought this product. She must have been embarrassed because she was looking down at the counter, her long hair hanging down over her face.

"The checkout girl was a southern gal with big hair and a neckline that was a little too low. She picked up the box of Tampax and looked for a price tag as she snapped her gum.

"'Honey-child, do you know what the price of this here Tampax is?' the checkout girl asked in a loud southern drawl.

"The girl shook her head and dropped it even lower, so her hair totally covered her face.

"Price check. Tampax. Price check. Tampax," the checkout girl called over the loudspeaker as she checked her fingernails and chewed her gum, her mouth wide open." Through-out the conversation, I was mimicking the check-out lady to the woman next in line, out of view of the salesclerk and young girl.

"The girl behind me started to snicker and I turned around and had to hold my hand over my mouth for fear of laughing and embarrassing the poor girl standing in front of us.

"A male employee's voice came back over the loudspeaker. 'Do you want self-adhesive or the kind you insert with your thumb?'

"The girl in line behind me and I looked at each other and, in unison, said, 'Self-adhesive?'

"The checkout girl muttered, 'Self-adhesive. Hmmm. Self-adhesive?' She leaned into the loudspeaker. What are you pricing?

"He responded, 'Didn't you want the price of thumbtacks?'"

The audience laughed, and I noticed my warning light was blinking. I was having fun and I didn't want to leave the stage, but my time was up.

"I haven't laughed that hard in a while. You were great. Worth the $100 tip," Nancy said as we walked to the registration table.

"Don't worry. I'm not quitting my day job," I said, laughing.

We counted the ticket money and completed our paperwork. Then we started cleaning up as the show drew to a close. We went back into the contest room just as the producer was announcing the final tally from the audience.

"We have a winner," he said. "Not only will this person get a 1983 Funniest Person t-shirt, but a three-to-five-minute video that will be shown on Showtime between movies. What a career boost that will be! And the winner is: Kathryn Gruhn. Come up here to get your prize." I was shocked. I wanted to run, but everyone was staring at me and clapping. Slowly, I entered the stage.

He greeted me with a big smile. "Give her a hand," he said as he handed me the microphone.

"Thank you for voting for me. This is quite a surprise. I'm very grateful," I told the audience.

The producer escorted me off the stage and said, "Let's get those papers signed."

"Wait a minute. I can't. My husband is a new doctor here in town. He just joined the Nalle Clinic. Can you imagine what he'd say if we were watching a movie on Showtime and a video of me telling jokes about Tampax popped up? No. That won't do," I said shaking my head. "I'm sorry."

"You have to sign the papers or I have to disqualify you."

"Nope, can't do it. Give it to the next person."

The producer grabbed one of his team members and asked who got the next highest votes. Then he went back on stage. "There's been a mistake. We miscounted the ballots."

Would you believe it? The runner-up was the man who told Nancy and me that 'women weren't funny unless they were fat, ugly or potty-mouthed.' He gave us both a 'told you so' look.

Nancy and I looked at each other and burst out laughing. We knew something he didn't. The truth.

Where's Your Nuts?

I have nostalgic memories of my mother making sticky buns for every holiday, a tradition that I have carried on for my own family. Holidays were the only times my family would be honored by my mother's sacrifice and her dedicated proof of brilliance. Sticky buns were my mother's way of telling us how much she loved us. She was feeding us, heart, body, and soul. I feel the same way. The local bakery can't match the taste of homemade cinnamon buns fresh out of the oven.

After the McCall family, who lived down the road, had a house fire, I had the urge to make sticky buns for them. What better way to tell them that I loved them? Handing them something that smells of warm cinnamon and caramelized sugar is as good as wrapping them in a cashmere blanket and brewing them a cup of hot British tea.

I grabbed my large bread-baking bowl that allows the dough to rise to its fullest height. This was not as easy as it sounds, given that I was nine months pregnant with our second child and big as a beached whale. I rubbed my belly before pulling my organic, ground white baking flour out of the cupboard. The McCalls would enjoy the fluffy, melt in your mouth, yet doughy texture, of my mom's sticky buns.

When the dough was mixed and ready to be kneaded, as always, I felt a sense of companionship—the dough tells me when it's finished by its elastic feel and appearance. I pushed forward with my palms, plunging my whole body into it, which always reminds me of the downward-dog yoga pose. Dipping my hands in cool water, I formed the dough into a ball, again thrusting my whole body into the dough. I felt 'kneaded' as I interacted with this masterpiece that never fails to change before my eyes.

I warmed the oven, turned off the heat, and placed a moist cloth over the top of the large bowl before placing it inside. Then I waited for the magic to come forth as the dough doubled in size. I was imagining how happy the McCalls would be to receive this fragrant, delicious gift.

A few hours later, it was time to flour the baking board and plop the dough in the middle. Placing a small pat of butter on my palm, I greased every part of my hands. After pushing and pulling the dough into a rectangle about a quarter of an inch thick, I brushed the dough with warmed butter, then dusted white sugar between the rolled-up layers of dough, along with a healthy sprinkle of cinnamon. I spread an equal measure of light brown sugar and butter, a quarter of an inch thick, on the bottom of the baking pan to create the caramelized, stick-to-your-teeth, dripping-when-warm and crunchy-when-cooled effect that encases the rolls and completes the whole experience.

After another two hours, the sticky buns had doubled in

size. I placed them in the oven and called Mrs. McCall to let her know that, in an hour or so, I'd be on my way with warm sticky buns from the oven. I hoped the bun in my oven would be popping out soon! I was already two weeks overdue.

"Oh, they're Dr. McCall's favorite. He especially likes the pecans on top," she said.

"Pecans?"

"Yes. We can't wait. See you soon."

I looked at the clock. I could make it to the grocery store, buy pecans, and be back in time to take the rolls out of the oven. No problem. Pecans, here I come.

I pulled into the parking lot and ran in to the Harris Teeter. Well, more like waddled quickly, since I was ready to deliver my second baby, Jennifer, any minute. I went straight to the baking section in aisle ten, but couldn't find any nuts. Frantically, I hurried from one aisle to the other, looking for pecans.

Two teenage boys were stocking the shelves on aisle twelve. I huffed and puffed up to them. "Where's your nuts?" I asked. "Hurry, I can't wait. Tell me. Where are they?"

The younger one looked dumbfounded and the older one began to chuckle.

"I only have a few minutes," I said. "Hurry! My buns are burning. Show me!"

"Are you looking for peanuts, walnuts, or pecans?" the older boy asked.

"Yes. Pecans. I need them for my sticky buns and they're in the oven right now."

191

"They're in aisle eight on the right side on the top shelf," he said, as the other boy walked away to hide his laughter.

I found the pecans, checked out, and ran to my car. When I entered the house, the sweet aroma of the sticky buns let me know I'd made it just in time to pull them out, turn them over, and let the caramel dribble down the sides. I sprinkled the top with pecans. Dr. McCall and his family were in for a treat.

While the buns were cooling, I had an 'aha' moment, and realized why the stock boys didn't understand at first what I was asking. There I was, a woman, nine months pregnant, screaming about sticky buns and demanding to know where their nuts were. The McCalls got a great laugh along with their delectable homemade rolls when I told them the story. My mother would have been proud of the sticky buns, but not my faux pas.

For Chrysler's Sake

One day not long after Bill, my husband, our two daughters, and I had moved to Charlotte, I received a call from a woman named Martha, who lived in a development called The Cloisters. We were living in an apartment nearby while our house was being built. Martha was looking for another child to join the ten-mile carpool to the school in which I'd recently enrolled Alice, our second grader. The headmaster at this private school had given Martha my name and telephone number. He thought it would be a good idea for me to meet other parents, since we were new to the school. Martha had two junior high school girls, Ashley and Winston, and her next-door neighbor had a high school-aged son, Clay. I was thrilled, because I wouldn't have to carpool every day.

Martha invited me for tea and snacks, so I could meet her and Clay's mother. I didn't realize at the time that this was really an interview to see if I made the grade. When the day came and I was heading out the door in a pair of jeans, a t-shirt and boots, my babysitter, whom we called Mama Lib, looked at me and asked, "Have you been to The Cloisters?"

"Can't say that I have, but I'm sure I'll be able to find it."

"That's not why I'm asking. The Cloisters is a very nice neighborhood and I know for a fact that the ladies won't be wearing jeans and t-shirts. They'll be dressed nicely. You know how important a first impression is," she said in her sweet southern drawl.

"Oh. I see. Okay, I'll go and change. No problem."

I came back in a skirt, blouse, panty hose, heels, earrings, and a necklace. My hair was curled and I'd spent a bit longer on my makeup, more than my usual five-minutes. I swirled in front of Mama Lib and smiled. "Will this do?"

"Why, you look very nice. Yes, that'll do."

"My husband, Bill, says that I accomplish metamorphosis in minutes. I go upstairs as a caterpillar and come down as a butterfly." I laughed. "Is there anything you'll need in order to take care of the girls while I'm gone? Alice is independent, but I know the baby, Jennifer, is needy."

"Yes. Where's Jennifer's blanket?" she asked. "I don't want to be searching for that right before naptime."

"It's in the dryer. I had to wait for her to go to sleep last night in order to wash it. You wouldn't have looked there. Good thing you asked. I'm going to drive out to the construction site to give the contractor who's building our house a check, and then, I'll be on my way to The Cloisters."

"Don't be late! Remember, they're checking you out."

"I won't." I glanced at my watch and I had a couple of minutes to spare if the traffic wasn't bad.

The contractor was right on time— I'd be early for my meeting at the Cloisters. As I was driving down the driveway of our beautiful farm, I couldn't help but admire the new barn my husband had built in his spare time. We had worked so hard removing all the cedar trees to make posts and had cut down numerous oak trees for fencing. It was a four-rail white fence that lined the driveway.

Rounding the corner, I noticed there was a new horse in the pasture with my horses. A week earlier, a young girl had stopped by while I was at the barn, and asked if she could board her horse with me for a couple of months. I told her that we hadn't divided the pasture yet, so she would have to turn her horse out alone at nighttime and bring him into the barn early each morning. He couldn't share the pasture with my horses, because there was a strong possibility they would fight. One of my horses, Snapshot, was the dominant herd leader and needed time to get used to a new horse. She agreed to meet with me and learn the ropes before bringing her horse, and we set up a time.

I jumped out of the car to get a closer look. Sure enough, it was the young girl's horse, Booker. I recognized him from the picture she showed me when we first met. I couldn't believe she'd just dropped her horse off in our pasture without notifying me or my barn help, who cleaned the stalls and turned out the horses.

I was not a happy camper. I jumped back into the car to go to the barn to call and tell her to remove her horse. I was about to start the car when I heard screams and pounding hoofs. Her horse had singled out Snapshot from the herd and was kicking and biting him. I ran for the barn as fast as I could.

I grabbed a halter, a rope, and a bucket of feed. Trying to avoid the mud puddles, I ran out to the middle of the pasture where the horses were fighting. I got a halter on Snapshot and Booker came back after him with his teeth bared. Snapshot dragged me through the mud as he tried to get away. I was swinging my rope and throwing feed to distract Booker. Again, he came at Snapshot. This time, I got dragged in the other direction, breaking my necklace and a heel on my shoe.

I dropped the feed bucket, which distracted the new horse. That gave me enough time to get Snapshot into the barn. When he was safely in his stall, I looked at my watch. I was going to be late for the carpool meeting! I ran to the car, sped the whole way, and arrived fifteen minutes late for tea at The Cloisters.

I ran up the long, slate sidewalk and rang the doorbell. As I was waiting, I straightened my skirt and noticed that my feet were covered in red Carolina clay. Should I keep my muddy shoes, even though one had a broken heel, or should I take them off and go inside barefoot? This was a tough question. I decided to take them off.

When Martha came to the door, she paused and looked me up and down. I followed her eyes and realized my dress was ripped on the left side and my nylons had so many runs and rips that one of my shoeless feet was completely bare except for a few chunks of red dirt.

"I had a confrontation at the barn with a horse. Kinda got a little messy," I said. I wiped my feet over and over again on her beautiful welcome mat as she kept staring at me. She probably knew she would have to buy a new welcome mat because Carolina clay stains.

"That's fine . . .Come on in. The other mom is eager to meet you."

Her beautifully decorated home could have been featured in *Southern Living* magazine. I turned the corner and entered the formal living room. The other woman was dressed to the nines, with a pedicure, a manicure—everything 'cured'. She looked as lovely as Martha. It was obvious they were both older than I, but plastic surgery had taken about ten years off their ages.

"Hi, so glad to meet you," I said. The look on her face was priceless. She was so taken aback by my appearance that her mouth was wide open. It would have taken a crane to shut it. I surely wouldn't have been able to tell that she was shocked any other way. Facial expression was nonexistent.

"Sorry, I had to break up a horse fight. I could have said it was a bar fight!" I laughed, but there wasn't a sound from her. Not even a smile. I passed by a mirror on my way to a winged-back chair and saw that I had mud clumps all over my face and neck, which made it look like I had some deadly disease. Measles, chicken pox, herpes? That's what happens when horses kick up their feet and spray you with wet Carolina clay.

I walked by the gourmet food and grabbed an extra napkin from the table to clean my face, but it was hopeless. As I walked, I heard the ding of something hitting the marble floor. I realized it was a bead from my broken necklace. I bent down as graciously as I could to retrieve it, and beads began to drop out of my blouse, underwear, and every nook and cranny, all rolling in different directions. As I stood up, my coifed hair fell to the front and partially stuck to my dirty face.

"Don't worry. The maid will clean up and return the beads to you," Martha said.

"Oh, it's a really cheap necklace. No need," I said, as I looked at her exquisite jewelry.

"Where is the maid? Maybe she could take a mop to my face," I said, as I continued to clean myself, trying to lighten the mood.

I guess it worked. Or something did. I made it through the interview and the women decided I was okay after all.

We set a schedule. I had Mondays. I would start the next day. All I heard from Martha while leaving was, "Don't be late."

"Don't worry. I won't," I answered as graciously as I could

On Monday morning, I drove my ten-year-old Chrysler LeBaron to The Cloisters, with my daughter Alice in the front passenger seat. The Chrysler was our first car, and we had ordered it from the factory. Against the car salesman's advice, Bill had insisted on a stick shift. The car wasn't designed for a manual shift and it was difficult to drive, but I was used to it.

We arrived at The Cloisters a little early and I watched the kids as they came out of the house. It's amazing what you can learn from a person's expressions. If, that is, they haven't had plastic surgery.

I rolled down the passenger window as the three of them approached the car. "Hi! I'm Kathy. I'm carpooling today. Don't worry, I'm not stranger danger," I said.

"I'm Ashley," one of them said. She took one look at my car and rolled her eyes. "You've got to be kidding. We're going to ride to school in that? No way! Your husband's a doctor! Where's your Mercedes or BMW? He IS a doctor, right?"

"Ya, I married a doctor. But for some reason you can't drive a medical school loan, so this has to do. Okay? Get in. It'd be a long walk and I can't imagine what the humidity would do to your hair. And which one of you is Winston and which is Clay?" I asked. Two children in the back seat were unaccounted for. One was a girl and one was a boy. Would someone really name a girl Winston? Like the cigarettes? Surely not. Well, I was wrong.

"I'm Winston," the girl said, then looked out of the window and totally ignored me.

"I'm Clay. Glad to meet you, and thank you for driving us to school."

Well, one out of three with manners wasn't bad. The kids didn't say a word after that. I could tell they weren't happy. Then Alice turned to me and said, "What's a Mercedes? I know what a BM is."

Her comment broke the ice and the kids started laughing. As we neared their school, I heard the two girls whispering. Then Winston piped up, "We want to be dropped off at the bottom of the hill. We'll walk up to the entrance."

I wanted to ask her why she was named after a cigarette, but instead I said, "Can't drop you off there. It's dangerous and I'll get in trouble. You'll just have to ride in my car until we reach the entrance at the top of the hill."

I knew they were embarrassed by my car, but I thought they needed to develop a little more respect. So, as I started up the hill, I pretended the car was having trouble and I messed with the clutch, which caused the car to jerk. I kept my other foot on the gas pedal and continued to rev the engine. All the students and faculty walking by us stared.

Ashley and Winston unbuckled their seat belts, ducked, and crouched on the floor. I couldn't help myself. "Don't touch the floor," I said. "The dog puked and pooped all over it and I haven't had time to get it to the car wash."

They screamed and instantly sat back in the seat. Then I was even naughtier. "Oh, by the way, my husband is concerned about your safety and so next week I'll be bringing football helmets for you to wear while you ride with me. Sorry about what it'll do to your hair. But safety first." The girls were quiet, but I could hear Clay chuckling.

The girls bolted out of the car at the entrance, slammed the doors hard, and gave me a dirty look. I laughed all the way home.

That night the phone rang. "Hello, this is Martha from The Cloisters. Ashley and Winston were concerned about having to wear football helmets to school next week," she said in her sophisticated Charleston drawl.

"Oh, Martha, I just made that up. The girls were making fun of my car. I thought that, if I told them they had to wear football helmets and then showed up next week and said I was kidding, they'd quit complaining about my car not being fancy."

"The girls were complaining about your car? I'll talk to them about that. I can assure you that they will be on their best behavior from now on," she said firmly.

The girls lived up to their mothers' promise and soon we all looked forward to meeting every week. I gave them motherly advice, and my jokes and stories were a hit. At times, even Alice got in on the act. But, poor Clay, the only boy, had to listen to four girls talk the whole way to school. Then again, maybe it was the most important education he would get for the rest of his life.

Welcome Wagon Striptease

My mother taught me to bring comfort food to people who have just moved into the neighborhood and for neighbors who are having bad luck. So, when I heard that a new family had moved to my street, I decided to bring them a homemade apple pie.

I was happy to know that the Washingtons had a little girl the same age as my daughter, Alice. All of her current playmates were boys, and active ones at that! Dr. Washington would be a wonderful companion for my husband, who was also a doctor. I wanted to make a good first impression and let them know I was just kitty-corner from their house. If they needed anything, I was there to help.

While the pie was cooling, I took a shower, curled my hair, applied makeup, and put on a cream-colored dress covered with bright red hibiscus flowers, along with nylons and pumps with a small heel. I found jewelry that matched, then headed out the door with my pie in hand.

There was no walkway from the street to their front door. I had to cross over their freshly seeded lawn, which was covered in wheat straw.

Kathy Thorson Gruhn

I rang the bell, and just as the door opened, I felt
something tickle me under my dress.

"Hello, I'm Dr. Washington," our new neighbor said as
he held open the door. "Come on in."

All of a sudden, I felt a pinch. No, a sting! I started
hopping up and down.

"Here," I said, quickly handing him my pie and swatting
my hind end. "Oh, my, I can't stand it!"

Yet another sting on my derriere propelled me to leap
forward. "Sorry, I can't wait."

I tore off my shoes and grabbed the right toe of my
nylons with my other foot, yanking so hard my knee flew up,
almost hitting Dr. Washington in the crotch.

"I have to take my clothes off," I yelled.

As I lifted and fanned my dress, Dr. Washington watched
me with his mouth hanging agape. How could he know I had
yellowjackets stinging me all over my body?

Fortunately, his wife came and poked her head around
her husband. "What's going on here?" she asked.

"Yellowjackets. I must have stepped on a nest when I
walked across your yard."

"Follow me to the powder room," she said.

The minute the bathroom door was shut, I yanked off all
my clothes down to my underwear. As yellowjackets
swarmed all around me, I swatted them with the hand-
embroidered towels from the towel rack. There I was, making
a mess in my neighbors' brand-new bathroom. Bug guts were
everywhere. My mascara and lipstick were smudged, and bee
parts were hanging from my hair. I was a mess.

"How's it going?" Mrs. Washington called through the door.

"I think I've killed all the yellowjackets."

"Are you allergic? Need Benadryl?" She paused, then asked, "Is the pie for us?"

"Yes, I wanted to bring you something special." *Was that a chuckle I heard?*

"Come out when you're ready," she said.

After I got my clothes on, I peered around the bathroom door. Dr. Washington was still standing there, holding my pie. "Sorry I destroyed your powder room."

"Glad to know it was bees under there. I didn't know what to think when you arrived at my door lifting your dress, tearing off your nylons and screaming, 'I can't wait' while you swatted your hind end."

"Welcome to the neighborhood!" I said sheepishly, my face red.

"We surely won't forget you! By the way, what kind of pie is it?" Dr. Washington asked.

"It started off as apple, but now I believe it's humble pie."

Living in Weddington

Zip It Up

Our younger daughter, Jennifer, was growing up right before our eyes. How could she be going on her first date already? My husband, Bill, met the young man at the door. I was watching from the kitchen, wondering how this would go down. Fathers tend to be a little protective of their daughters. Bill, a physician juggling a crazy schedule, wasn't the most active father, so I wanted him to feel he was the boss on this one.

"Come on in," Bill said.

The boy sheepishly came through the door and waited at the bottom of the stairs like a lost dog. Bill was studying him intensely. The style at the time was for boys to wear pants at least one size too large so that they hung down, often to the point that their underwear was showing. The ghetto look, I was told. Bill circled around the boy, staring at his pants. The next thing I knew, Bill was taking off his belt.

"Here, you forgot your belt. You can use mine," Bill said, threading his belt through the belt loops on the boy's pants. The poor kid was so embarrassed he didn't say a word. Before Bill buckled the belt, he grabbed the pants and lifted them up to the boy's chest. The poor thing was still speechless. Then Bill cinched the pants tight. I don't know how the kid could breathe.

I ran up the stairs to Jennifer's room. "Hurry, your dad just took off his belt and put it on your friend's pants. I don't know what he'll do next. You better get downstairs and fast."

Jennifer ran down the stairs, grabbed her friend's hand, and went out the door with a "Bye, Dad." I guess the two of them had a nice time. I never saw the kid again, but he did return the belt.

As I watched Jennifer enter the world of romance, I reflected on my first crush, Mr. Espinda, my sixth-grade teacher. He was so handsome and 'cool,' as my generation would say at the time. I would stare at him and take in his every movement. This tall, dark, debonair man from Hawaii was so exotic, a far cry from the blonde, blue-eyed Scandinavians from my hometown in southern Minnesota. I scribbled hearts in the corners of my notebook and wrote M.E. (Mr. Espinda) plus Me inside them.

My crush on Mr. Espinda did not keep me from talking in class, however. One day, exasperated, he called out, "Zip your lips, Miss Thorson."

This made me laugh, which only increased his frustration. After all, I had earned my nickname, Chatty Kathy. That's why I had to sit in the first row, so I wouldn't disturb the other students.

"To the front of the room. Now!" he said, pointing to a spot next to the blackboard. I pranced up there, appreciating the fact that he was giving me special attention—the naïve thought of a twelve-year-old girl.

He walked over to where I was standing. My excitement that he was within two feet of me was more than I could bear. I distinctly remember the smell of his cologne.

"Get closer to the board," he said.

I inched closer, my toes only a few inches from the wall. He drew a small circle about an inch above my nose.

"On your tiptoes, and put your nose on this circle, and don't move. You can stop when I tell you to."

I looked at him in disbelief, but did what he asked. After a couple of minutes, my calf muscles started cramping. Tears began to stream down my face. I looked over at Mr. Espinda, but he didn't even glance toward me. Had he forgotten about me? Was he enjoying the fact that I was in pain?

I turned and looked at the class and a few students started to laugh. I smiled despite the tears and embarrassment. As I was turning back towards the board, Mr. Espinda's eyes caught mine. My nose was off the board. There was a moment of uncertainty. What was he thinking? Where was this going?

After an awkward pause, he quietly said, "You can sit down now."

I hung my head to hide my tears and plopped into my desk chair. How could he do this to me? Opening up my notebook, I was strictly business. I scribbled through the M.E in all of the hearts. The crush was over.

The next day, I came prepared to stage a joke. I pulled out a skirt zipper and taped it across my mouth. Then I turned around in my seat and faced the class. The kids began to laugh knowing I had been told by Mr. Espinda to 'zip it up' the day before.

Little did I know that Mr. Espinda had walked into the classroom. When I turned around, he was standing right in front of me. He took one look at the zipper and said, "Up to the board."

Oh, no! Not again. Would I ever learn?

Thinking about Jennifer's first date, I wondered what my strict sixth grade teacher would have thought of 'ghetto look' pants. Would Mr. Espinda have told that boy to "belt it up?"

Mel and a Helicopter Chase

I was excited when I found out that *The Patriot*, starring Mel Gibson, was being filmed in Brattonsville, South Carolina, which was less than forty miles from my home. What an opportunity to get an autograph or at least a glimpse of the actor!

A few days later, I saw an ad inviting people to bring their horses and try out to be an extra on the set. This was my chance for a moment of fame, and I was going for it.

On the morning of the audition, my daughter Jennifer stopped on her way out of the door. "Mom, my science project is too bulky along with my bookbag. Will you drop it off this morning on your way to work?"

"Sorry, honey, I'm going to South Carolina with my horse to see if I can be an extra on *The Patriot*. It's a movie with Mel Gibson and they need riders. I took a vacation day at work."

"I want to go!" she begged.

"You have school and your horse is lame. No way."

"Mom, you know I'm a reporter for the school paper. I'll tell the principal that I'm going to write about the film and get some pictures. She'll let me leave early, and I bet Morgan would let me use her horse."

"Get to school. You're going to be late."

The next thing I knew, a horse trailer was coming down my driveway. I went to the barn. Ya, it was Morgan's horse. Then I saw a cloud of dust at the top of the driveway as Jennifer drove her car toward the barn.

"What are you doing home?" I asked.

"I'm going with you to the tryouts for the film. I told you, I'm going to write up something for the school paper."

"I can't believe they let you out of school for this. It wouldn't have happened when I was your age. Okay, get the horse cleaned, braided, and looking spiffy. My horse is ready."

"I know all about when you were in school. You walked uphill coming and going."

We headed towards Brattonsville and stopped at a gas station close to the area for directions to the location.

"You ain't gonna get in there," the clerk behind the counter said in a slow southern drawl. "Why, they have copters flying overhead, and they moved all the power lines. It's crazy. They have all the roads blocked with cops. You ain't getting nowhere near that place. I'm tellin' ya now." He took off his hat and pulled his hankie from his back pocket to wipe his brow. "It's hotter than Mama's boiler."

He gave us the directions anyway, and we found our way to the entrance. Four highway patrolmen, along with a number of guards, were lined up at the gate. I checked in and gave them our information and were given strict instructions not to go anywhere else except the grounds where the tryouts were being held.

I came to a driveway I thought was the entrance and saw a man putting a watermelon in his garden. I was confused. I watched him a little longer and realized I had taken the wrong drive and was at a private residence.

"I've seen people take a watermelon out of a garden, but I've never seen anyone put one back," I yelled out of my open window.

The man started laughing. "Busted! I'm having people over for dinner and I wanted the garden to look great. They've never been to a southern farm. Can I help you?"

"Ya, we're lost. My daughter and I are supposed to try out for the movie with our horses and we got this far. The highway patrolman told us to take the next driveway into the field. I guess we didn't take the right one. Do you know where it is?"

"Yes." He chuckled. "You take the next driveway on the left. It'll get you there."

"Thanks. You've been a big help. Keep up the good work in the garden," I said, and we both laughed.

I took the next driveway into the field and pulled up to the horse trailers. I looked around and no one was in riding attire. Our horses were clipped and braided, and Jennifer and I looked as if we were ready for a formal hunt. The people around us—all men—were long-haired, bearded, scruffy, and wearing old Civil War coats. Their horses looked as if they hadn't been groomed in ten years.

"What's with your get up?" one guy asked. "You look funnier than hell. We're reenactment people. You're trying out for the wrong movie. I think you're looking for *National Velvet*."

We ignored them and saddled up our horses. We rode around the field to warm up the horses. Then I saw a guy loading a cannon and getting ready to fire it.

"Jen, head back for the trailers now! They have cannons and guns. We are at the wrong place. We'll be in the next county if our horses hear a cannon." I turned my horse Snappy around with Jennifer right behind me. We headed for the trailers and quickly loaded both horses.

Just then, a truck drove up and an old man rolled down his window. "Where you girls off to? You just got here for the tryout," he said.

"We aren't dressed right, our horses are too fancy and we certainly wouldn't be safe with cannons, guns, galloping horses . . .Anyway, I need to go because my daughter Jennifer is upset. She was going to write an article about the movie, but that isn't possible now. Thank you for asking."

I looked more closely at the man. "Hey, you're the guy with the watermelon trick whose driveway we went down."

"Yes, that's me. I own this property. All six hundred acres. Well, I think you girls look great. These people are crazy and I don't like the fact that I've been taken over by Tinsel Town. I'm supposed to have this guy named Mel Gibson to my house for dinner. Don't know anything about the guy. My wife is all excited. I think it's a bunch of hooey."

"Mom, did he say Mel Gibson?" Jen asked.

"Yes, he did." I turned back to the man and said, "You've been so gracious and I want to thank you for saying we look wonderful."

"If you want to come back tomorrow, I can give you a tour. Maybe Mel Gibson will be here. I'll help your daughter write a great story."

"Mom, did you hear that. Can we? Pleeease?" Jen asked.

"Are you sure? You aren't too busy?" I asked.

"Nah, you're my kinda folk. Gotta help you," he said.

"That would be great. Sorry to be in such a rush. It's just that they're getting ready to set off the cannons and our horses will go crazy. See you tomorrow."

We sure had a happy ride home. It hadn't been a wasted trip after all. Tomorrow, we'd get a private tour. Jennifer would get information for her newspaper story and we might see Mel Gibson. Whoopee!

The next afternoon Jennifer and I headed back to Brattonsville.

"Mom, I'm so excited. I told everyone at school today that I was going to meet Mel Gibson and get a story," Jen said. "I was told that he wouldn't even give an interview for the *Charlotte Observer*. Wow, I'm really lucky."

"Well, Mel probably heard your mama calling it the *Charlotte Disturber* and the word got around. No wonder he refused." We both laughed. "You ARE very lucky, indeed."

This time, I knew exactly where the farm was located. I pulled up to the same check station. There was a car ahead of us and I could tell that the people were trying to get in. It was clear the officers weren't going to let it happen.

One of them walked up to our car. "Can I help you?"

"Yes, we have an invitation from the owner for a private tour and for my daughter to get a story for her school newspaper," I said.

"What's the man's name and where is the invitation?"

"Oh, my, do I feel silly. I didn't even get his name. You see, he was putting this watermelon back in his garden and then we were trying to find the tryouts for the horses and—"

"I'm sorry, ma'am, you need to turn around and go back home. This property is off limits to everyone. We're just doing our job to protect the film company and their property."

"No . . . really . . . we . . ."

He turned and walked away without even giving me a second look, much less letting me finish what I was saying.

"Oh, no. The kids are going to make fun of me at school. I won't have any story. I'm going to be so embarrassed. They'll think I was lying," Jennifer said. I could tell she was about to cry.

I checked out the blockade. There was just enough room to get around on the right side if I kept two wheels in the ditch. I gunned the car and took off.

I had an invitation. I just didn't know the man's name or address. I was sure I could find the farm. No one's going to stop me from getting my daughter to her appointment. NO ONE! I thought as I put my pedal to the metal.

Jennifer was looking out of the back window. "Mom, the police officers are waving their hands in the air. I don't think we're supposed to go."

"Never mind. Just act like we know where we're going. We have an invitation, you know."

"But you don't know the guy's name."

We heard a roaring sound. Jennifer rolled down the window and looked out.

"Mom, mom! There's a helicopter coming! I think it's headed for us!"

"They wouldn't send a helicopter after us. I'm sure that's the filming crew."

Within seconds, the helicopter was right above my car, hovering. The whirl of the blades was deafening. I kept flooring my 1996 Acura Legend. What a great car!

All of a sudden, I saw the house about a half a mile ahead. "Hang on, Jen. I see the farmhouse. I'm making a run for it."

I heard muffled sounds coming from somewhere, but I couldn't tell if they were coming from the helicopter or my car motor. Plus, I was concentrating on my driving. It was difficult to keep the car on the soft, sandy road at such a high speed. I swerved into the driveway and ran the car right up to the house. The man I met yesterday was on the front steps. He was on the phone. The helicopter was straight overhead. I got out of the car and yelled, "It's my daughter and I. Tell them not to shoot!"

The man covered the mouthpiece on the phone. "Oh, it's you. Yes, come on in. Wow, did you give the police a workout. They were asking who was coming to visit and said that the person had a formal invitation. That threw me off. If you'd told them that you were the girls on the horses yesterday, I would have known immediately who you were."

"They didn't let me get that far. I'm sorry, but I don't even know your name," I said.

He laughed, gave me his name and address, and then proceeded to talk to Jen. "What do you need for your newspaper story?"

"Well, I was hoping to get an interview with Mel Gibson."

"You don't want an interview with that grump. He came to dinner last night and I could tell he didn't want to be here. We have some photographs and his autograph in a notebook. Come in the house and I can show you more."

We went inside the man's old Victorian farmhouse. It was large, quaint, but not overly fancy. I felt as if I'd stepped into my own childhood home. We went into his living room. There were photographs and books on the coffee table. We sat on the couch and he handed me a small notebook.

"He wrote some notes in here, too. You can have these. Will that do? He gave us photographs that they use for newspaper articles." He added, "I'm also going to take you on a tour of the set. Come on and get in my truck."

The first place he took us was the food and wardrobe tent. Jennifer took pictures as we walked through. Then he took us to the campgrounds where the actors, horses, and trailers were located.

Our next stop was a large brick building that looked like it was partially burned. From behind, we could see that it was a false front with no sides or back. "Here, have a souvenir," our farmer friend said as he grabbed a brick from the building and handed it to Jennifer.

Then we walked over to an area of the field with mounds of grass that reminded me of the mounds of snow in the dead of winter in Minnesota. "These are the so-called 'bunkers' that the cavalry shoots from and the horses fall into. They shoot the cannons from here, too. It's wild and noisy. Fires burning. I can't believe those horses ride right through that stuff. The horses are special trick horses that fall on command. I saw them practicing yesterday. They have to have a vet here in case one gets hurt. It's the law."

Jennifer took more pictures and wrote down everything she heard. By the time we were finished, she had dozens of pictures and all kinds of information for her story, along with the photographs and notebook our kind host had given her.

We thanked the man over and over for his help and the wonderful tour. He drove us back to his house and we got in our car.

"Mom, I can't believe you outran a policeman AND a helicopter," Jen said.

"Piece of cake. You needed your newspaper story and I wasn't going to let a stupid misunderstanding get in the way." I guess all those years of speeding in my old Tornado, and even those thirteen speeding tickets, paid off. We both had a grin on our face all the way home.

Voodoo for You

I'm not one to believe in the supernatural. However, I have a true story to tell that may make believers out of all of us.

In the early days of my marriage, before I had children, I went to visit a high school friend who was living in New Orleans, Louisiana. I was teaching in Rochester, Minnesota, where I grew up. My friend Paulette thought I needed to see a different part of the country and identify with the artsy-fartsy part in me that I hid from everyone. So, during a weeklong vacation from teaching, I went to stay with her.

Now, many years later, the eerie painting depicting Bourbon Street I bought from an artist on that trip reminded me of the dichotomy between life in New Orleans and the life I was living in mainstream Southern Minnesota. Walking through the French Quarter, I saw spaghetti and alligator wrestling and unusual bars as I munched on Cajun food. The antique shops looked like something out of the movies *Halloween* or *Friday the 13th*. Every day was a new adventure. Paulette wanted to give me a different experience, and we drove out of the city into the bayou where the country folk live. As we made our way through the swamps and self-built homes, we came upon a little shack. Paulette said we needed to go inside and meet the Voodoo Lady. I burst out laughing, but she was serious. She made me promise to be polite, and not laugh or she wouldn't take me inside. It would be difficult for me since I poke fun at almost everything, but I agreed.

The outside of the place could've been mistaken for an enclosed food stand like we had up north. However, the hanging shrunken heads, animal skulls, alligator parts, snapping turtles and voodoo dolls let me know this was no food stand. Paulette rang the bell at the counter to let the Voodoo Lady know we'd arrived. Out from behind a tie-dyed curtain came a woman about four and a half feet tall. Her black skin was weathered, a bandana covered her hair, and her speech was difficult to understand due to her missing teeth and her dialect. She played with her necklace of bones and feathers as she eyed us up and down. I stood at attention. It was hard for me to determine her age, but something told me she was an old soul.

I felt sorry for the woman, so I bought a voodoo doll which sported four different colored pins. She explained the power of each pin, but I didn't pay attention. I had no intention of ever using it. I just wanted to pay her for the entertainment her store provided. As we were leaving, the woman said, "That voodoo doll is not to be used for evil. It has great power."

I had to bite my cheek, so I wouldn't break into laughter and embarrass my friend. When we got in the car, I was laughing so hard that I started coughing. Paulette looked at me and smiled, but she didn't laugh. She just shook her head.

That voodoo doll stayed in the same brown grocery bag from day one. It managed to make it through five moves, finally landing in my attic in Charlotte, North Carolina. I kept it in a memorabilia box along with the family photos and diplomas. As I was going through the boxes after our move, I was trying to figure out what to do with the voodoo doll. I didn't have the heart—or the guts—to throw it away and didn't want to take it to the Salvation Army either. It stayed in a crumpled grocery bag in a plastic bin in the attic. I forgot all about it.

Years later, when I was working as a speech therapist, I wanted to raise money for a child who needed hearing aids. I knew how to put on a horse show, and thought this would be a great way to make $6000 and have fun while doing it. The family of the young girl didn't have money to purchase the hearing aids and were happy and thankful that I would help them. I put out a call for volunteers, which would reduce expenses. A woman named Robin offered to send out the mailing list, and to collect the entrance fees. I was so grateful, because this freed up my time to get the Knights of Columbus show grounds ready. Also, time to order ribbons, paint the jumps, and secure volunteers to help on the day of the show.

Three weeks before the event, my girlfriend Christi called. "Hey, Kathy, I just received a mailing for a horse show on the same date you told me you were having a horse show."

"What are you talking about?"

"There's a horse show scheduled at Robin's farm, not the Knights of Columbus, on the same day you told me you were putting on a horse show. The mailing doesn't mention anything about raising money for hearing aids for that little girl."

"What? Tell me the date again," I said. "There must be a mistake."

There was no mistake. The woman who'd graciously offered to send out the mailing—which were addresses from an established horse organization that I'd been given permission to use—had instead used the list for her own gain.

I couldn't believe it. With such a limited time frame, there was no way I could retrieve the list, mail out the correct invites or inform people that there was a mistake. I was devastated. Not for me, but for the family who was expecting hearing aids for their daughter. I didn't have $6000, nor did I know anyone who could pay that amount. The reason I was holding the fundraiser in the first place was because neither insurance nor school funding would cover the expense. I called the volunteers, show grounds, judges and cancelled the show, while staring at the expensive box of show ribbons.

The night before the horse show, Christi came over to console me. My husband was at a medical conference and fortunately knew nothing about this. I didn't tell him, because he would've caused a stink. We were meeting new friends in the horse community and I didn't want the reputation of being a troublemaker.

I was crying, and Christi was trying to think up ways to let people know how evil this woman was. I don't know if it was the word *evil* or the wine, but I suddenly remembered the voodoo doll in the attic. I ran upstairs for the paper sack and pulled out the doll. At the very least, I needed to have some fun and get my mind off the horse show.

"Christi, come upstairs and into the master bedroom. I have something to show you," I said. I was already laughing. Christi met me in the master bathroom. I handed the doll with the plastic bag of pins to Christi.

"What's that and what are the pins for?" Christi asked.

"It's a voodoo doll. And I have no idea what the pins are for," I said.

"Didn't it come with instructions?"

"I'm not so sure the lady who made this could read or write."

"Where'd you get it?" she asked.

"In New Orleans, years and years ago. The Voodoo Lady told me to never use it for evil."

"Really?" Christi laughed. "You don't believe that, do you?"

"Naw. It's just a doll with some pins, but I need something to cheer me up. Let's have some fun."

"What does this red pin do?" Christi asked as she took the pin out of the bag and stuck it into the black cloth doll with human hair and hand-stitched arms and legs.

"Let's not do that. Just to be on the safe side." I grabbed the doll out of her hand and pulled the pin back out.

"You're scared of this thing."

"Well, if you saw the place where I bought it and the look on the women's face—and heard what she said to me—you'd feel the same way. Let's think of something that wouldn't actually hurt anyone," I said.

"Well, it would be good if Robin got too sick to put on the horse show," Christi said.

"Naw, what if she got sepsis and died? I'd feel awful. I've got it! We won't use the pins. I'm going to get a Barbie doll and the Breyer horses out of the kids' toy box to represent Robin and the horse show and put them in the shower with the voodoo doll. We'll ask the voodoo doll to make it rain, so Robin will have to cancel the horse show!

"Fabulous!" Christi said.

We laughed as I turned on the shower in my master bathroom and drenched the Barbie doll along with the appaloosa, bay, and gray Breyer horses. The voodoo doll sat on the edge of the bathtub watching the whole ordeal. We said some abracadabra-like stuff and chuckled between every made-up string of gobbledygook as if we were a couple of witches cooking up a brew. I needed the laughter. When Christi left, I slept like a baby. I didn't even wake up when my husband came home from the medical meeting in the wee hours.

The next day, the phone rang at six in the morning. My husband groaned and asked who would call at this hour. It must be an emergency, I thought, quickly picking up the phone.

"Did you hear? Do you know what happened?" Christi yelled into the phone.

"Christi, it's six o'clock in the morning. What the—"

"The horse show was cancelled. It got rained out. In fact, the rain washed away Robin's riding ring. Did all kinds of damage. Do you believe that? That frickin' doll worked!"

"Holy crap. You can't tell anyone about this. Promise," I whispered. I could hardly breathe. I was in shock. Bill was disgusted that he was awake so early in the morning and had gotten out of bed and headed for the bathroom.

"I've got to go. I don't want Bill to hear. Bye." I hung up the phone just as I heard Bill open the shower door.

"Were the kids playing in the shower with their Barbie dolls and horses? And what's with this other doll?" Bill yelled from the bathroom.

I jumped out of bed and ran to the bathroom. Bill had already taken Barbie and the Breyer horses out. I grabbed the voodoo doll from the edge of the bathtub. I didn't want my husband to even touch the voodoo doll. I was spooked.

"Sorry, I forgot to clean up," I said, not wanting him to blame the girls.

Later that day, I placed the voodoo doll in a nice box. I explained to her that she would have her own place in the backyard. I put in a cookie and a piece of jewelry, and buried the box in the very back of our property. I didn't want this thing pissed at me.

Years later, I tried to sell that three-acre parcel. It wouldn't perc, the soil test failed, even though the land all around it could support a septic system. The developer that I sold the land to, was able to buy a strip of land that did perc next to the road adjacent to the parcel. Just the other day, out of curiosity, I looked at the map of what became a fifteen-acre development. Every piece of property was subdivided into sellable lots, except a small quarter acre at the very back that was designated as green space, even though this wasn't a conservation development. Yes, that designated green space is right where that voodoo doll is buried. That quarter of an acre is all hers.

And the little girl who needed the hearing aids? I was able to sweettalk a company into selling me a pair at cost for $1500.

How did I pay for it? It just so happened that Bill had given a speech at the medical meeting and the sponsors sent an unexpected honorarium of exactly $1500 to our home address. It was made out to him, not his business. He was happy to let me use it for those hearing aids. I never understood why that check came to our home address, or why it was made out to my husband and not his medical corporation. A check never came that way before or since. Maybe the voodoo doll had something to do with it. I'll never know.

No Comfort Food

I love to cook and gather family together for the holidays. It reminds me of my own childhood, and I don't feel a bit guilty about eating all that comfort food. Between immediate family, cousins, and friends, we usually have twelve to sixteen people for dinner. It's a blast. I set the table with our wedding china and listen to the stories. The laughter is worth all the cleaning and cooking. But I have to say, I had no idea that a Thanksgiving dinner would end up as a story. I think this memorable one was in 2000, but don't quote me on that.

The first call of the season was to our firstborn. "Hi, Alice, we're planning on Thanksgiving dinner and want to know what your plans are. Oh, you're going hiking on Thursday. How about if we get together on Friday?" I jotted this in my notepad. "You're vegetarian now? When did you start that? Okay. No problem. I know how to cook for vegetarians. See ya on Friday."

"Bill, Alice is now a vegetarian. I guess she's following in my family's footsteps. So, no meat for her and no gravy. I'll make the stuffing vegetarian. And by the way, we're having Thanksgiving on Friday."

"Friday's fine. And that's a wise, healthy choice. Good for her," my husband answered, with his nose buried in the morning paper.

Alice called me right back. "And no marshmallows on the sweet potatoes. They have gelatin, you know, they're made out of horse hooves."

"Oh, please don't say that to someone who has horses. But okay. No problem."

Next, I called my other daughter, Jennifer.

"Hi, I 'm calling about Thanksgiving. We've changed dinner to Friday. Will that work for you? . . . You want to bring a new friend? No problem." I put a check next to her name. "What did you say about your friend? He's allergic to nuts and shellfish? Okay, no problem. I can accommodate that. We'll see you Friday." I jotted the *no nuts and no shellfish* next to the *no meat, no gravy and no marshmallows* already on my notepad.

"Hey, Bill, Jennifer is bringing a NEW male friend to Thanksgiving. I guess she's still in the 'catch and release' program. So, we need to make sure there's no nuts or shellfish on the menu because he's highly allergic."

"Is that a problem?" he asked.

"I'll just leave the pecans out of the sweet potatoes. I can't have marshmallows on top anyway."

"Why no marshmallows?" Bill asked.

"They have gelatin in them. Please don't ask me that ever again," I said, looking out at my horses grazing in the pasture. "I love s'mores!" I started singing "Girl Scouts together, that is our song, winding the old trails, rocky . . ." Boy, this menu will be rocky, I thought to myself.

Alice called me back and wanted to know if her friend Leah could come and bring her family. I grabbed my list and added their names.

"Oh, Mom, they're vegan, so no dairy," Alice added.

"No dairy? Exactly what does that entail?"

"No butter, no eggs, no milk, no cheese, and nothing made with those products."

"Okay, I'll work on that," I said. I wrote *no butter, no eggs, no milk, and no cheese* next to the *no shellfish, no nuts* and the *no meat, no gravy, and no marshmallows.* I wasn't too concerned. I would use margarine instead of butter, and none of the recipes called for cheese. I could grind almonds as a substitute for milk. Oh, wait, no nuts.

I called Alice back. "Can I use goat's milk? Is that considered dairy?"

"Yes, Mom. Just think of it this way. If an animal produces it, you can't use it. Okay?"

"Okay." I was trying to wrap my brain around that one. "I can figure it out."

Then I called my friend Annie, who had just moved to town. I couldn't imagine her spending the holiday alone.

"Hi, Annie. I'm wondering what you're doing for Thanksgiving. We're having dinner on Friday instead of Thursday. Would that work for you?" I asked. "You can come? Great! . . . You can't have wheat? You have celiac disease? Can you have any grains?" I asked as I added *no wheat* to my list next to the *no butter, no eggs, no milk, and no cheese* and the *no shellfish, no nuts* and the *no meat, no gravy, and no marshmallows*. Oh, my! I said to myself.

The last phone call I made was to my cousin who was flying in from California to see us. She had tentatively planned to come for Thanksgiving and I had to find out for sure if she would be there.

"Yes, I would love to come. I can't wait. But I have a request. I'm on a diet and I can't have sugar or nightshades. You said you changed the date to Friday. Right?"

"Yes. It's Friday. I know what sugar is, but what are nightshades?"

"Any root vegetables. No potatoes, sweet potatoes, carrots, onions, rutabagas, beets. Those kinds of vegetables. If it grows underground, I probably can't eat it. It doesn't go with my blood type," she said.

"Okay . . . hmm . . . all right. I'll make it work. Can't wait to see ya," I said. Blood type?

I added *no sugar, no nightshades* to my *no wheat, no meat, no gravy, no marshmallows, no butter, no eggs, no milk, no cheese, no nuts, and no shellfish*. I then compared it to my Thanksgiving menu. No sticky buns, no dressing, no bread, no butter, no turkey, no gravy, no sweet potatoes with pecans and marshmallows, no potatoes, no cream of soup, no onions, no pumpkin pie, no eggs or sugar in any of the dishes. That leaves me with peas . . . beans . . . mushrooms. Wait, is that a nightshade? Lettuce . . . unsugar cranberries . . . and tea. Oh, my!

Bill put down his newspaper, stood up, and looked at my list. "That'll be a challenge. Oh, by the way, the doctor said I needed to reduce my salt intake and my cholesterol."

I stared at him for what felt like a long time. I couldn't help myself. I was having a meltdown.

"Oh, nooooooo problem," I finally said. "We're having hot water soup, unsweetened iced tea, peas and cardboard sandwiches. Wait, are peas high in sugar? Oh, well, everyone will be healthy and happy. I'll have dinner prepared in a jiffy and I'll have time to ride my horse, who has so far avoided being turned into a marshmallow. I'm giving up on the comfort food menu this year." I headed to my Indian cookbooks for help. Thank goodness they had made it through our many moves over the years.

My Thanksgiving menu was:

Homemade Tofu Turkey with Low Salt Soy-Sauce Gravy

Pepper and No-Salt Salt

"Smart," Heart Healthy Margarine

Organic Rice

Curried Broccoli and Cauliflower with Coconut Gravy

Green Salad with No Nightshades and Homemade Citrus Dressing

Fruit Salad Sweetened with Agave

Dark Chocolate Sauce Sweetened with Stevia over Gluten Free, Nondairy Ice Cream

Herbal Iced Tea (Alice likes decaffeinated)

AND it was a low cholesterol menu, which thrilled my husband. Also, no alcohol, in case someone had recently joined Alcoholics Anonymous.

I was able to pull it off and the food was delicious. The stories were great, as always. And I learned how to accommodate friends and family with different eating requirements. Who says an old dog can't learn to cook new tricks?

Delaying Retirement

Mountain Shenanigans

Have you ever seen an unsuspecting man in a compromising position with a donkey? Well, I have, and it was one of the funniest predicaments I'd ever witnessed. I'll never forget this vivid picture of my husband as I looked out my kitchen window at our mountain house one windy day in late fall. There was Bill, running as fast as he could downhill in our back pasture as he tried to lift the legs of our donkey, Chip, off his shoulders. When he saw tiny Chip at an auction, he thought this innocent-looking donkey was so cute that he bought him. Well, apparently, Chip thought pretty highly of Bill, too. I guess when Bill turned to go down the hill after feeding him some potato chips, little Chip fell in love.

Bill was brushing off his shirt as he entered the house. He went straight to the kitchen sink, where he washed his hands furiously. His face was covered in sweat and he wiped his brow with one of my clean dish towels.

"What happened? Are you okay?" I asked, playing dumb. I wanted his side of the story.

"I don't know. I guess Chip realized he's a man. He tried to mount me."

"I'll call the vet and fix that in a hurry. No more deals from the auction barn. Okay? And what about the other white donkey? He's bigger. Good luck getting him off your back."

"Okay. But you have to admit Chip's cute. I'll take the white donkey back to the auction barn."

"Yeah, Chip's cute alright, but now he's horny, too. Can I trust you to just take the white donkey back and don't bid on any so-called 'deals'?"

"No problem."

I watched the next morning as Bill hauled away the white donkey and left Chip in the pasture by himself. He was baying and running alongside the fence the whole time the truck and trailer were going out the driveway. I wasn't sure which one he was missing, Bill or the white donkey. Poor Chip. I thought the trauma had ended until later in the day when I saw Bill's truck and trailer came back down the drive. There in the trailer were fifteen adult goats. THAT MAN JUST DOESN'T LISTEN.

Out the door I went. "And what do you have in the trailer?" I asked, as he rolled down his window.

"Dairy goats. I'm going to make cheese and butter. They were cheap. A real deal."

"Bill, that story sounds familiar. Like when the guy showed up from Idaho with five yaks and you had the idea of breeding the yak bull to our angus cattle and selling 'yattle' meat. Ya, that worked until you named all the yaks and they became pets. And don't forget how, when our angus heifers saw that yak bull, they went through the fence in total fear.

You got mad when I renamed it 'skedaddle' meat. The neighbors thought we'd lost it. 'Where'd you get those hippy cows?' they'd ask me. Now we're in the dairy goat business? Really? And who's going to milk them every day? You're a doctor and I'm a speech pathologist. We work!'"

"I'll figure it out. It's not your problem."

"Yeah, it always ends up being my problem," I said, as I caught one of the goats by her collar to adjust her bell. I looked at her more carefully. I wasn't familiar with dairy goats, but I had enough vet knowledge to know an aged animal when I saw one. I pushed back her lips and there were no teeth. This goat was old. Really old.

"Bill, let me guess. These goats were reaaaally cheap."

"Yep, I was lucky."

"Well, you just bought a defunct dairy herd. They're so old that they can't have babies anymore, which means they can't produce milk. Look at her teeth. My guess is that they're all old. The joke's on you! Plus, goats can get out of any fence. I had pygmy goats and they took their horns and ripped right through the fence wire. And they eat anything in sight."

"Hmm. Okay. I'll take them back tomorrow," he said reluctantly.

"Thank goodness! And I'm going with you."

The next morning was glorious. I was disappointed that I'd be spending half the day at an auction barn watching old men in bib overalls spit tobacco, but I'd survive. Again, I looked out of the window. There in Bill's rose garden were twelve goats. The flowers and leaves were gone and only the

three-foot stems were left. All one hundred roses were
stripped clean. I heard Bill coming down the stairs. He was
dressed in khakis, a nice polo shirt, and leather shoes. I didn't
have the heart to tell him about his roses. I would herd the
goats back in the pasture and break the news gently at a later
time.

"You're a little over-dressed for the auction barn, aren't
you?"

"I have a friend coming over to get some wood for his
fireplace. Then I'll change. By the way, I've been meaning to
tell you that I think we should save money by not buying
paper towels. We can use rags to clean. That's what my
mother did," Bill said nonchalantly.

"Excuse me. What did you say? Clean up doggie do-do
with rags? Is that what I heard?" I couldn't believe my ears.
Was he losing it? He surely wasn't thinking about saving
money when he bought those old goats, even if he did pay
bottom dollar.

"Sure, I'll be glad to cut up some rags for you, but I'm
keeping my paper towel stash."

I looked out the window and saw a brand-new Chevrolet
truck pull up to the shed. The door opened and a
distinguished man in khakis and a white, ironed shirt stepped
out.

"My friend's here," Bill said, as he started out the door.
"It won't be long. I work with him in the clinic and I want
you to meet him, but first change and take your hair out of
that bun. It makes you look old."

It was a good thing he was walking out the door. Let's see. First the goats, then the paper towels and now, the bun. I was getting a little annoyed. I know, after thirty years of marriage, you tell it like it is, but Bill was going a little too far in my opinion. Then I heard the revving of the motor of our John Deere tractor.

I looked out the window, which always seemed to be the bearer of bad news, and there was Bill driving up with a new log splitter in tow. He must have been hiding it behind the barn. I hadn't seen it before. I wondered how many paper towels it would take to pay for that log splitter. Now my blood was beginning to boil. I watched as he pulled up to the logs that we had cut and dragged out of the woods for the past month. The same pile that had given me a bad case of poison ivy. I was taking cortisone pills as if they were candy. Stayed awake for a week and ate everything in sight. Watching him cut the logs, split the wood, and stack it in the back of his friend's truck bed made me angry. Khaki Number Two stood and looked around as Bill worked diligently. His buddy wasn't getting his hands dirty. Ya, it was time to put my hair down and meet this guy.

I pulled a nice top out of the closet and combed my hair. As I was mulling, I couldn't help but count the ways I was pissed. I was going way back. Yaks, donkeys, goats, paper towels, hair bun, log splitter, poison ivy, and a pompous ass, and I don't mean another donkey. I was going to meet this guy alright. I was sorry he was going to be the brunt of my anger. I couldn't scream or create a ruckus. That would make

ME look bad. I had a better idea. Don't mess with a woman that's got a good imagination.

I went to Bill's closet, pulled out his coveralls, a torn paint shirt, his tall snake boots, and a straw hat full of holes. I was letting my hair down alright. I dressed and looked in the mirror and there was something missing. But what? Billy Bob teeth! Yes, from my Halloween costume. The fake teeth that appear as if I had one tooth in my mouth. Perfect!

I grabbed a rope and an old aluminum washtub and out the door I went. I passed Bill as he was busy with his log splitter and walked up to his friend. I had a flashback from the movie *Cold Mountain* with Nicole Kidman, the part where she was going to catch the rooster and roast him in the pot. With my back to Bill, I gave his friend a big, toothless grin. Bill had no idea I was wearing my Billy Bob teeth. I'm not sure what he would've done.

"Howdy, I'm Bill's wife," I said. "I'm gonna catch me a goat and roast him in a pot. Do ya want to stay for supper?" I looped the rope over my head as if I was a rodeo queen. He didn't say a word. Just shook his head no.

"Don't mind my wife," Bill said, not even glancing my way, "she gets a little dramatic at times."

"I put my hair down for ya, Bill, so I'd look reeeeal purty," I said in my best southern drawl. I leaned in and whispered, "It makes him real hot." I smiled and winked at his friend as I watched him wince. *Oh, I'm so naughty!*

I walked away saying, "Gonna catch me a goat and put 'im in a pot, gonna catch me a goat and put 'im in a pot." I headed for the gate to the pasture. Placing some rocks in the washtub, I shook it thinking I could fool that goat into trying to eat the 'grain'. Then, as she put her nose into the tub, I'd put the rope around her horns and tie her to the gate.

That goat took one look at me, dropped her head, and bolted towards me. I panicked and used the washtub as a shield. When the goat hit, she was stunned by the sound and I was able to get the rope around her horns and drag her to the fence post. I wrapped the rope around the gate post and tied it. I was just as shocked as the goat. I couldn't believe I pulled that off. That's when I realized this was an old, ornery billy goat, and not a nanny.

I turned around and our guest's mouth was wide open. He quickly thanked Bill for the wood, jumped in his truck, and was never seen again. I can just imagine the story he told his wife when he got home.

It was time to round up the remaining goats and get them out of Bill's roses and back to the auction barn. All in a day's work at "Gruhn Acres"—the place to be. Yeehaw!

Piggy, Piggy

Bill and I were adapting well to being empty nesters. The house was quiet and our schedules were just that, our schedules.

My daughter Jennifer, who was a sophomore at the University of North Carolina, was living outside of Nashville, Tennessee, training her horse with an accomplished rider for the summer months. She took a break from riding, and was on her way to St. Louis to meet her boyfriend's parents for the first time. She had conversed with them on the phone, but this was the first in-person meeting. When she called me to tell me where she was going, I reminded her of proper etiquette, greetings, and areas of conversation to avoid. Neither of us could have anticipated what would happen next.

At one point while she was on the highway, Jennifer followed a tractor-trailer full of baby pigs. She saw their little snouts and hooves protruding through the metal crates, and it just touched her heart. She grabbed a tablet that was on the passenger seat, wrote a note, and drove next to the truck driver's window and held it up: *Can I have a pig?* The truck driver read the sign, smiled, nodded, and pointed to the next exit sign.

He drove off the ramp into a truck stop with Jennifer following close behind. He got out of the truck as she approached him. "You can have one if you're willing to crawl into the back of the truck and grab it," he said.

"No problem," she said, as she scrambled into the back of the truck. A few squeals later, "Piggy" had a new momma.

"What does he eat?" she asked, as she held the tiny, white piglet. "And how old is he?"

"Anything you eat," he said. "And they're all about five days old."

Laying the sweet piglet in her lap, she continued on to St. Louis. She arrived at the suburban house and admired the manicured lawn and flowers, with lush gardens nestled against the tidy brick house. Dogwood trees graced the edges of the freshly painted entrance, and large oaks framed the house to perfection. She found an old horse blanket in the back of her car, placed Piggy in it, walked up the sculptured sidewalk, and rang the doorbell.

"Hello, come on in. We've been so looking forward to meeting you. You're just in time for dinner," her boyfriend's mother said, as she greeted Jennifer at the door. "Do you have luggage? I'll get my husband to help you carry it in."

"Glad to meet you, also. I don't need help. I have a small suitcase and I can handle it myself," Jennifer said, as she looked around at the white carpeting and polished furniture.

"I have a favor to ask. Would it bother you if I brought in my pig?" Jen asked.

"Oh, cute. You have a stuffed pig."

"No, it's a live baby pig. It's just a few days old and very sweet. I think it's housebroken, because when I take it out in the grass, it goes potty right away, and doesn't leave a mess in the car. Isn't that amazing?"

There was an awkward pause. "No, and no . . . I'm afraid not. I don't want a pig in my house."

"My mom wouldn't care," Jennifer said, and then remembering my etiquette lesson, added, "Well, it's early summer and not too hot, so I guess it can live in the back of my Honda for a couple of days. The car is seventeen-years-old and really cheap, so Piggy can't do that much damage. I have to find some food, though."

"I'll find some scraps for you," she said.

The relationship between her and her boyfriend's mother improved over the weekend. The pig lived in the car and Jennifer won the family over despite her new four-legged friend.

Sunday night, Jennifer headed back to Nashville, Tennessee, where she was working with a trainer to become qualified for the A Pony Club rating, which would give her top certification in the care and training of horses. I had taken her horse, Irish Whip, to Nashville two months earlier with the truck and horse trailer.

Jennifer finished the training on Monday, and I was on the way from Charlotte with the horse trailer to meet her and bring Irish Whip back home. I had no idea Jennifer had added a pig to her 'family'.

I received a call from Jennifer late that afternoon. "Mom, go ahead and check in at the Holiday Inn where you made the reservation. I'm sure you're tired and I'm running late. Have the clerk hold a key for me and I'll show them my license, so I can get in. I have some packing to do."

"Great! It's been a long drive and I want to take a hot shower and relax. I like that idea," I said.

After my shower, I turned on the TV and crashed shortly thereafter. I didn't hear Jennifer enter the room or feel her crawling into the king-size bed. In the middle of the night, I heard some short snorts. I looked around the room with the help of the dim light of the moon. Jennifer appeared to be sound asleep. She must have been snoring a little, I thought. I went back to sleep.

More snorts woke me up. I sat up and saw something moving under a horse blanket on Jen's side of the bed.

"A rat! Jennifer! Wake up!" I said, as I was standing on the pillows pinned up against the headboard and wall.

"Hush, Mom! It's just a pig. He must have to go to the bathroom. He's housebroken."

"Oh . . . ya. Just what I thought. A pig in the Holiday Inn that needs to go potty." I couldn't believe my ears or eyes. There was this little, white Yorkshire that was sleeping on my bed.

Jennifer wadded the pig up in the horse blanket and started to head out the door.

"Where are you going? You can't just walk by the reservation desk with a pig in a blanket," I said. "Oh, that's a good one. A 'pig in a blanket.' Just what they're bred for."

"Funny, Mom. This is how I got him in the hotel. And he's not dinner."

"I wasn't being funny. I'm serious. There's no fee for keeping a pig in your room. I don't even want to ask. We're going to get kicked out."

"I'm sure there has been worse things in this place. I'll go down the back stairs if that will make you feel better."

"Nothing will make me feel better at this time. Wait . . . how did you get . . ." She was out the door before I could finish my sentence. I watched from my window as she let the pig out of the blanket at the back of the parking lot. It went to the bathroom. Then it scampered around, jumping up in the air and making 180 degree turns. I was trying to process what I was seeing. A pig? Really? We're known for rescuing horses, dogs, cats, rabbits, and birds, but this took the cake.

When she came back to the room, and I tried to question her, she said, "Mom, I'm tired. I'll explain later," as she gave the pig some water.

"I would say so. Lots of explaining. Good night . . . oh . . . what's his name?"

"Piggy. Go to sleep, Mom."

We packed up in the morning and snuck the pig out of the hotel. I had an extra stall in the barn at home, so I wasn't too worried about keeping her pig. We drove to the barn, and as we loaded the horse, I noticed the pig was getting quieter and lying down more frequently. I knew this wasn't normal for a baby pig, since I had spent time catching them myself in my younger days. The horse was in the trailer and Jennifer followed me in her car with the pig fast asleep on her lap.

When we stopped at a gas station, I asked, "Did that pig sleep in your lap the whole way here?"

"Yes, he's so sweet."

I watched the pig as he wobbled and fell down.

"What are you feeding that pig?" I asked.

"Pizza. It eats what I eat."

I knew that wasn't the nutrition a piglet needed. It was too young to eat solid food, but I didn't have time to stop and get the proper feed. I had to get home in time to go to a funeral. I was on a strict schedule. My schedule.

Once we were back on the road, Jennifer would pass every so often and point to the sleeping pig on her lap with a big grin on her face. She was falling in love with that little guy. When we stopped again for gas, the pig was even weaker.

We headed down the road and I started to think that the pig wouldn't make it home. I was overcome with guilt, knowing that that pig was dying. I waved Jennifer over to the next exit and we stopped at a grocery store. I ran in and picked up corn meal, baby formula, and water. I had a large syringe in my truck for horse emergencies. I filled the syringe with the mixture and started to force feed the piglet.

There I was, sitting in a grocery store lot with a squealing pig on my lap, teaching it to suckle from a syringe in the middle of nowhere. Jennifer watched and helped.

"I hope I make it in time for the funeral. Come on. Let's go," I said.

Not much later, Jennifer pulled alongside of me. The pig was bouncing off the seat, dashboard, and floor. It was alive! Very alive—normal piglet behavior.

She pointed to the exit sign. We pulled off the road. Jennifer was yelling from her car window and I rolled my window down. "I think he has to go to the bathroom. I have to let him out. He's nuts!" She said as she was getting out of the car.

"No, he's normal. That's what they're supposed to be doing." I looked at my watch. "We aren't going to make it back to the house and then to the church. We're going to have to change here and go straight to the funeral." Now I was on the piglet's schedule.

We made it to the church just as one of the last cars was parking. I pulled to the back side of the parking lot hoping no one would see me, but my big, dual-wheeled truck with a twenty-eight-foot trailer wasn't something I could hide. I pulled the window doors down on the trailer for the horse, placed the pig in the dressing room, and headed to the sanctuary with Jennifer running behind me.

Every so often during the service, I could hear her horse neigh. The church was in downtown Charlotte, nowhere near a farm. I could see people looking around. I guess they assumed a child had a toy that made horse sounds. That's what I would like to think, anyway.

When the service was over, I tried to get to the trailer as fast as possible, but when I heard squealing sounds coming from the dressing room of the trailer, I knew that pig had to go potty. "Not here," I said to myself. "No, not here!"

Yes, here. The pig had to go. People were coming up to the trailer and petting the horse, while I herded a pig around the grassy area. I wanted to tell them my last name was Clampetts from the *Beverly Hillbillies* show. Anything but my real name.

Piggy never did make it to a stall in the barn. He lived with my daughter in her bedroom for the rest of the summer. He had his own personal kennel. She bathed him, took pictures of him, dressed him up, and slept with him in her bed, his little, white head on his own little, white pillow. He loved the dogs and he fit in with all the other crazy critters in the house—animal and human.

More Piggy, Piggy

Jennifer fell in love with a white Yorkshire pig that was cute and cuddly as a baby. She had rescued it off a truck headed for the feeder lot when it was less than five days old. Not something that I'd do, but admirable on Jennifer's part. She named him Piggy and he lived with us for the summer.

I was raised in a rural area and believed that you never name an animal to be slaughtered. Piggy had a name. It was a dilemma.

When Jennifer first brought him home, I thought he should live in the barn. He never made it there, because from the moment she discovered he was smart enough to be housebroken, Jennifer thought his rightful place was in her bedroom. Piggy lived in a crate when he wasn't sleeping with her. Yes, she has a picture of his little head on a pillow next to hers. Cute.

When it came to our dogs, Piggy ruled. Pigs are smarter and gutsier than dogs. My golden retriever, husky mix, and Carolina dog were terrified of the pig. In fact, Piggy is the reason I now understand why, when someone eats too much, they're referred to as a hog. Food was Piggy's passion and his reason for being here on earth. He was a hog, in more ways than one! There couldn't be any dog food anywhere if the pig was out of his crate. He would squeal, bolt, and bulldoze his way to the food as the dogs scattered and quivered in a corner. As the pig reached twenty-five pounds, he grew even more devious about being caught.

By this time, I'd realized that Piggy was a boar (a male pig) and would eventually grow to weigh around 900 pounds. And he'd grow tusks. Not a safe pet for anyone. Hogs can bite and plow you down. I know. I helped out at a pig farm when I was young. This was a problem that I didn't discuss with my daughter. The idea of Piggy as a full-grown boar wasn't in Jennifer's reality. And Piggy on a barbecue? No way.

A month went by, and as Piggy grew, Jennifer was preparing for an internship in Ecuador through the University of North Carolina. This seemed like the perfect opportunity to wean her from the pig and find another place for Piggy to live. Not that this would be easy. When she left for the weekend to visit a friend, she gave me strict instructions on how to take care of Piggy. I knew she was testing my babysitting abilities before she left him with me for three months. Piggy stayed safe in his crate and when he squealed, it was bathroom time. I could handle that.

That same weekend, I was holding a special luncheon for members of the Mecklenburg Medical Endowment. We were meeting to organize an auction to support charities in the Charlotte area. Twelve women were coming to my house, and I had hired a caterer to prepare the meal. Before this special event, I polished the silver, set the dining room table

with my fine china, and prepared mimosas. We were bringing
in top-notch donations and I was on a roll. We started off in
the living room. After our meeting, I escorted the ladies into
the dining room. I went back to the living room to gather the
notes, and that's when I heard the first grunts and squeals
coming from Jennifer's room on the second floor. Oh, no!
That pig had to go to the bathroom. Not now! I said to
myself. I waited for a moment and he was quiet. But just as I
was walking into the dining room, I heard another squeal.
This time it was a little louder. I looked around. The women
were chatting away as the food was being served, and helping
themselves to a second mimosa. It didn't look like any of
them had heard the squeal. I figured I had just enough time
to run upstairs, grab the pig, and take him outside to pee
without anyone noticing.

I ran upstairs, grabbed Piggy, and out the front door we
went. I left the door open because he was very fast at finding
his bathroom spot, and I wanted to be able to hear what was
going on with my guests. Piggy sniffed for a second or two,
went potty, and took one look at me. I knew that look. It was
the devious pig look. The 'watch this' look. He tucked his
head and pulled his hind feet under his belly.

I crouched, ready for action. I figured he was going to
run away from me. The next thing I knew, he ran to the left
and then to the right—I was playing defense with a pig. He
plowed right between my legs and bolted into the house
through the open front door. He headed straight for the
kitchen, knowing full well where the dog food was located.

I ran after him as his little feet slid sideways on the polished wood floors. He was heading for the dog food bowl and the slippery floors weren't slowing him down. In the kitchen, he was sashaying around the cooks, evading me. Plates of food were falling, cooks were scrambling and when Piggy went for the human food, I managed to grab him. He squealed to high heaven and he wiggled away from me, heading straight to the dining room.

The physician wives screamed as the pig ran under the table, bumping into their legs. I followed him on my hands and knees, yelling obscenities. He was smart enough to stay just out of my reach. I lunged, tearing my dress in the process, and caught him by one leg. He was kicking and squealing his lungs out. If you've ever heard a pig squeal, it sounds as if they're being killed. They fake it because they're drama queens. One of the women yelled, "Don't hurt him."

He got away one last time before I cornered him between the bar and the screen door. Finally captured! As I picked him up and turned around, I saw twelve frozen faces, all with their mouths wide open. There was a long, awkward pause as they stared at me. I had food down the front of my torn dress—a disgusting combination of orange juice, asparagus, apple salad and chicken gravy. I was a mess. I wish someone had taken a picture. Now I would laugh like crazy, but it wasn't funny at the time.

One of the girls said, in her most gracious southern drawl, "Why, how cute. I've heard about those pet potbellied pigs, but I've never seen one. Honey, what's his name? He looks like Gordy from the movie. Oh, my. Can I pet him?"

"Of course, he's very friendly." I felt a little guilty about passing Piggy off as a potbellied pig, but at the time, I felt like it was the right thing to do. She gave him a pat on the head, avoiding the splattered food.

"Does anyone else want to pet him before I put him in his crate?" I asked. There were no other takers. So, I walked back up the stairs, saying a few naughty words under my breath to Piggy, which I think he understood because he was being as good as gold. I gave him a little motherly squeeze to let him know who was really the boss around here. He went docilely into his crate, but I'm sure I detected a smile on his piggy little face.

When Jennifer left for Ecuador, I found a neighbor to take Piggy. He had a farm full of pets and animals for his grandchildren. Unfortunately, Piggy had the whole farm of critters—animal and human—terrified of him. The last I heard, he weighed well over 200 pounds and his tusks had grown in. I never asked what happened to him, nor did Jennifer. She had come to her senses by the time she came home from Ecuador. In our minds, Piggy is still living on that farm.

Your Car's a Meth

"When it rains, it pours" is an old saying that is true at times. A flood of bad luck and misunderstandings can lead to a disaster, or, at least for me, a funny story. Finding the humor in a difficult situation is a great skill to develop, especially if you get yourself into as many crazy situations as I do. The upside is, it helps you get through truly challenging times.

In 2007, a tree hit our house and damaged the roof badly. This fifty-foot oak tree was healthy, but it lost a bet with a straight wind and landed on top of our house. My husband blamed himself. According to his story, he was studying different religions via books he ordered on Amazon. He was raised Christian, but he was wondering why there was so much discord between religions and wanted to know more about other faiths. He'd read books on Muslim, Judaism, and Hinduism, and was in the process of learning more about atheism. A storm was brewing outside as he sat in his office on the third floor of the house. He was ordering The God Delusion by Richard Dawkins and his credit card kept getting declined. On his third try, just as his card was finally accepted, he heard a tremendous boom. The house shook as the gigantic oak landed in the middle of the roof. Its branches broke through the attic, which was only a few feet from his office. Bill was so upset that he declined the book when it arrived in the mailbox days later.

The house destruction was tremendous because, not only was there damage to the roof, but a two-inch rain poured through the ceilings and flooded the walls. The sheetrock in every ceiling was bulging, and the light fixtures had small waterfalls. Our furniture, cabinets, and floors were destroyed.

Early in the morning, I called a restoration company called After Disaster to dry and clean up the mess. A crew of four guys came over right away. They ordered a storage pod, placed it in the driveway, and began cleaning and moving our furniture. They also cut the sheetrock in strategic places to drain the water. Bill and I were checking rooms and closets and packing up boxes of stuff to take to our mountain house, where we'd stay during the renovation.

Around 8 p.m., the head of the company came by to check on things. When he saw the bulging ceilings, he told us to quickly remove any important documents, jewelry and valuables and get out. It was dangerous to be in a house with ceilings that were ready to burst.

We rushed to gather our valuables and vacate the house. Bill was worried about his tools. We packed them in my car because it had a larger trunk, and he headed for the mountain house.

That left me with his BMW, which was an M3. I went to the garage with a laundry basket full of papers and jewelry, only to find that the ceiling had partially fallen on his car. I quickly started the car to back it out, forgetting it had a manual transmission. The car lurched and stalled. I cussed and restarted it and backed it out shortly before the whole ceiling caved in, filling the garage with soggy sheetrock, wet insulation, and dirty rainwater. I saved his car. Bill would be happy.

I went back in the house to let the After Disaster crew know that I was leaving. They were still working to save what they could. That's when I saw my piece of horse-hair pottery, which was shaped like an urn and had a beautiful lid on top. It was raku fired with a glaze that was decorated with hair from the tail of my horse, Snapshot, whom I had for twenty-five years. I'd been offered $40,000 for that horse. I turned it down, because I loved him. There was a special bond between us, and that pottery meant so much to me. I quickly grabbed it off the small table in the front hall as the sheetrock started to fall.

I pulled away from our house with a tear-stained face and a change of clothes, my husband's car stuffed so full of documents, photo albums, jewelry, and other special items that I had to drive with my horsehair pottery between my legs. By this time, it was almost midnight. I had a two-hour drive ahead of me, and I was exhausted as I drove north on Interstate 77. My mind was racing, trying to sort out the mess we were in.

I kept forgetting Bill's car was a manual shift, as I was used to driving my automatic, and I kept failing to use the clutch properly, causing the car to jerk and lunge. Not that I can't drive a shift, but I hadn't done it for a while, and my mind wasn't on my driving.

I made the turn to highway 21 and came to a stoplight in Elkin. Again, I forgot to shift and I hit the gas pedal when the light turned green. The car lurched, tossing me forward. The lid of my horse-hair pottery flew up in the air, hit the dashboard on the passenger side, and broke into pieces landing on the floor.

That was it. I had a meltdown. I burst into tears as I drove, wiping my face with my forearm. Snot was dripping down my nose. I tried to reach into the glove compartment, while driving, to see if I could find some Kleenex, but I couldn't reach it.

Instead, I turned on the inside light to assess the damage to my pottery. When I saw at least three pieces of the broken pottery lid, I cried some more. I missed my horse. I missed my house. I missed my children. I missed everything. I looked in the review mirror and saw my swollen eyes and red-blotched face. I cried even harder. I think I was emoting about every bad experience I'd had in my whole life.

That's when I saw flashing blue lights behind my car. I slowed down, but the police car didn't pass me. I was the only car on the road, so, obviously, the lights were meant for me. Bill was notorious for not putting the DMV sticker on his license plate. I hoped that was the reason for the stop. I wasn't speeding. I quickly turned the inside light off, not knowing if it was illegal to drive with it on.

It seemed to take the officer a long time to walk up to my car. I wiped my face with my sleeve again and tried to compose myself. I had my driver's license ready for him, and I rolled down the window when he approached.

"May I see your license, please?" he asked, as he shined his oversized flashlight in my face.

I winced at the bright light and handed it to him.

"I've been following you for a while and your driving is erratic."

"My driving is erotic?" I was tired and had mixed up my words. I've done worse. I asked for decapitated coffee at a Starbucks once.

The officer paused, probably trying to figure out where I was coming from. "You're swaying from side to side. And you're speeding up and then slowing down."

I guess he didn't think I knew what the word erratic meant, and I needed an explanation. My voice quivered and I blurted out, "It's because of my pot! I'll never be able to replace the lid." I broke down into a primal cry and looked longingly at the pieces of lid on the floor. "I'm so upset." My story was the truth, and it made sense to me, but I guess the highway patrolman heard 'pot' and 'lid' and he had a different idea what the problem was. He was able to get a good look at my red, swollen eyes with his oversized flashlight. The car was dark and he didn't see the piece of pottery wedged between my legs or the broken pieces on the floor.

"Out of the car and stand on this white line," he said, in a deep, demanding voice as he pointed to the line in front of the car.

I opened the door and carefully removed the horsehair pot from between my legs to carefully place it on the passenger seat. I guess I was taking too much time.

"Out of the car. Now!" he yelled.

I jumped at the tone of his voice, and headed in his direction. I stood on the white line. He asked me to touch my nose and walk on the white line with one foot straight in front of the other. Then he had another request. "Repeat the alphabet backwards."

"You've got to be kidding. It's after midnight and I'm tired. Can I sing it forward and then give you the letters backward? How much time do I have?" I asked politely. I could tell he was frustrated at my acing the agility course.

"Forget the alphabet. I need to see your registration."

We walked together around the front of the car to the passenger door. As I opened it, dog hair flew up in the air, causing me to sneeze. Now my face was a really big mess. I tried to wipe it with my hands. Bill kept his BMW clean on the outside, so that the other doctors at the hospital thought he had a great car. However, the inside was a mess. I often referred to his hotrod 1995 M3 as a BM-3 because the inside looked like crap! I kept hoping this would encourage him to clean it, but it only made him mad.

I was struggling to open the glove compartment with my sticky, wet hands when, all of a sudden, it burst open. Needles, bottles of liquid Novocain and gloves flew out with all the paper documents that were stuffed inside. Bill, a rheumatologist, kept a stash of extra supplies in the glove box because at times they would run out of supplies at the office.

The whole mess hit the floor on top of my broken pottery lid, which made me cry all over again.

"Are you on meth?" the officer asked, eyeing the medical supplies. I was a basket case at the moment. What I heard was "Your car's a mess."

I stopped what I was doing and looked at him.

"Ya. Sorry . . . this is not my car . . ."

Before I could say another word, he barked, "Back to my car. Now!"

He instructed me to sit in the front seat. He sat across from me with an intense look on his face, and pulled out his computer. I figured he didn't like to see dirty BMW's. Must be a man thing, I thought.

"Who's your provider?" he asked.

"My husband?" I said, thinking that the question was unusual.

"His name?"

"William Bryant Gruhn."

"How long has he been your provider?"

"About thirty years. More or less," I said, trying to do the math with half a tired, traumatized brain. "Wait, I think it's more than thirty. Let's see . . . 1976 . . . from . . . 2007. No, I need to subtract from 2000 first and then add seven years. I believe it's . . ."

He was typing in Bill's name as I kept trying to figure out how many years I'd been married. Then he exclaimed, "He's a doctor. Your husband is a doctor and he's your provider?" Looking back, the patrolman must have thought he had hit the motherlode. My husband, the methamphetamine provider for the entire Appalachian Mountains. Wow! His lucky discovery would be in the headlines of every newspaper nationwide.

"Yes, he works parttime. Kind of retired, but he wants to help the poor. The money is good." In my mind, I was shining a wonderful light on my husband.

"Yes, I bet the money is good. And he isn't helping the poor."

His comment upset me, but I didn't want to get him riled up any more than he already was. "Officer, I think everything was going well until you made the comment about my husband's car being a mess. I know how men like cars and…"

"I didn't say your husband's car was a mess."

"Yes, as I was looking for the registration, you commented on how messy my husband's car was."

"I asked you if you were on meth," he said impatiently.

"Meth? What do you mean?" I asked, trying to process what the word meant.

"Methamphetamine!"

"Oh . . . my gosh, no. Are you talking about the people on the billboards with the rotten teeth and acne faces? Look at my teeth! I'm not on meth. Look at my face. Okay, don't look. I look a little rough, because I've been crying."

Tears started welling in my eyes. "You see, a tree landed on my house, rain flooded it, and I broke the lid to my pot trying to drive my husband's stick shift. The very pot that was made from my horse's hair. I had him for 26 years and he died. I miss my horse. I'm not on meth—I'm a mess." I was wailing by this time. I leaned into him and almost laid my head on his shoulder for support. Fortunately, I stopped just in time. "Do you have some Kleenex or a hankie? Anything?"

"Pottery made from horsehair?" he asked, leaning over his console and handing me a Kleenex.

"Come with me to the car. It'll be easier if I show you."

We walked to my car as I blew my nose several times. I took my pottery out and held it up. "It's called raku. After the pot's been fired in a kiln, it's heated in a fire pit. While it's still hot you take pieces of the horse's tail hair and burn it into the glaze on the pot. It makes wispy lines and curls. See?" I said as I pointed out the lines on the pottery. "It's a keepsake."

"That explains a lot. When you said 'pot' and 'lid' I was suspecting drugs."

"Holy crap. I hate this car and this car hates me. It's nothing but trouble. The last time I was pulled over by a patrolman while driving this car, I was in my pajamas. My husband had overslept and he was going to miss his plane and I had to get my daughter dressed to take her to school. I didn't have time to dress myself before we left for the airport. After dropping my husband off, the car broke down. There I was in these flimsy pajamas, when, of all times, a patrolman stopped to help me. He insisted on driving me and my daughter to her school. I think he thought I wasn't safe dressed the way I was. Then I had to go into the school because Alice, my daughter, was late and I had to explain what happened. I was in my pajamas! It was humiliating! I hate this car."

There was an awkward pause. I had talked so fast and so long that the officer was probably trying to process it all.

"I'm sorry for your loss and this misunderstanding, but I don't think you should be mad at your husband for buying the car. It's a man thing. But it wouldn't hurt if he took it to a car wash." He smiled, trying to soothe my increasing agitation.

"You're right. I . . ." The officer interrupted me, no doubt realizing I could have him there all night in the unwanted role of a marriage counselor.

"I'll follow you to your home to make sure you're alright."

The patrolman followed me to our mountain house and turned on the blue lights as we drove down the driveway. Bill saw the lights and ran out of the house to see what was wrong. He ran up to my window and I rolled it down. "Are you okay?" he asked.

"It's your car's fault. Your car's a meth!" is all I could say.

About the Author

Kathryn Thorson Gruhn grew up in the small town of Blooming Prairie in southern Minnesota. She moved to the South with her husband in the late seventies and currently lives on a horse farm in Tryon, North Carolina. She has two grown daughters and three grandchildren, along with many four-footed friends.

Before becoming a writer, she was a speech pathologist for 35 years, working primarily with children ages birth to eight, which prompted her to create the *My Baby Compass* program. *My Baby Compass* is a program for parents and caregivers of children ages birth to eight that promotes the early identification of developmental delays and gives a parent the peace of mind that their child is on target for typical developmental milestones. She is presently in a joint venture to have a digital, interactive *My Baby Compass* format that is evidenced based. For more information, visit www.mybabycompass.com.

She is a bestselling author in the book, *Soul for Success*, and her selection received the Editor's choice award.

She has been telling funny stories for many years, and putting them into writing was one way she handled the grief of losing her husband of forty-three years. Her first book of funny stories, *Drug Tested for Being Happy,* was well received and her audience begged for more. *Drug Tested for Being Happy* is available on Amazon and Audible.

Kathy has signed a contract with Wonderlore/Studio South to create 'edutainment', to enhance educational activities through theatrical and digital presentations using the concepts of the *My Baby Compass* program. She is in the process of writing scripts with the Muppets for the first episodes in *Jungle Rules,* that will be performed in the Greenville Children's Museum for children from birth to eight-years-old. It is in the initial stages of production, so look for it in the near future. To learn more, visit, www.mybabycompass.com.

Her greatest pleasure is making people laugh through her jokes and stories. She performs her stories in a program, Piedmont Home Companion, to raise money for local charities. Follow her at: www.kathythorsongruhn.com for future events, books, and stories.

And yes, she is writing one more book of funny stories, *Oops, I'm Stuck!* . . . and that's it!

Acknowledgments

I would like to thank my readers, family and friends for such encouragement and help. A writer's world is a lonely place. It takes a village to create a book.

My writing group, Under Construction, which meets every Tuesday throughout the school year, has been invaluable to me. Suggesting titles for stories, critiquing content, and giving advice to help me improve my work is not only wonderful, but makes me accountable. My gratitude to Cheryl Boyer, Cindy Campbell, Doris Motte, Ginny, Mehltretter, Jennifer Hurlburt, Kathy Brown, Kim Love Stump, Lisa Otter Rose, Mary Struble Deery, Nancy Bischoff, and T.D. Taegel. I want to especially thank Bridgett Bell Langson and Lisa Batten Kunkleman for reading and editing my manuscript.

Ty Thorson, my brother, was the comma king and gave me valuable information on content. He also encourages me to quit playing computer bridge and finish my stories and projects..

Nancy Schofer, who loves to find mistakes in newspapers, was gracious enough to edit my first book and happily agreed to edit this one. I met her on a Dartmouth educational cruise with my daughter, Jennifer, and we became instant friends. She needs to create a sign: I work for books! since she lets me pay her with a box of these books. Most authors write for the fun of it, not because they make money.

Maureen Ryan Griffin, the instructor of Under Construction and an author herself, is my writing coach, editor, friend, and cheerleader. This book wouldn't be possible without her. She is the 'midwife' for many writers. We have spent many days and nights working on the My Baby Compass series, articles for magazines, chapters in books, but her favorite is listening to my funny stories and publishing them.

Jack Canfield, creator of the *Chicken Soup for the Soul* series, encouraged me to write another book of funny stories, and he put me in contact with Marci Shimoff. She is a $#1 NY Times Best Selling Author, International Speaker and Co-founder of *Your Year of Miracles* coaching program. Since she wrote, *Happy for No Reason*, I figured she may be interested in reading a book of funny stories. She was gracious enough to read my script and give me an endorsement. Thank you to both Jack and Marci.

I also want to thank the many friends and family from Blooming Prairie, Minnesota, who know me and my stories. Some were in the first book, *Drug Tested for Being Happy*, and some were fortunate not to be in this book. I have been friends with some of the characters since kindergarten, and we have continued to get together every few years since then.

I am currently writing my last book of funny stories, *Oops, I'm Stuck!*, and it will be published sometime in the next couple of years. But don't hold your breath.

If you like what you read, pass it on to your friends and family and give them a laugh, too!

Made in USA - Kendallville, IN
80399_9780984408566
11 10 2021 1203